A Parent's Guide to a Peaceful Home

Transformation Begins at Home

PATRICIA BRAXTON

Order this book online at www.trafford.com
or email orders@trafford.com

Most Trafford titles are also available at major online book retailers.

Illustrators: Paris Simone Brower
             Rachel Wilson

Printed in the United States of America.

ISBN: 978-1-4669-4200-4 (sc)
ISBN: 978-1-4669-4201-1 (hc)
ISBN: 978-1-4669-4202-8 (e)

Library of Congress Control Number: 2012911097

Trafford rev. 02/13/2014

www.trafford.com

North America & International
toll-free: 1 888 232 4444 (USA & Canada)
fax: 812 355 4082

To God, Mom and Dad, Kimberly J. Braxton Brower, Eric Brower, granddaughters Asia and Paris, Teacher's Administrators, Eunice Kennedy Shriver, and all my children.

Table of Contents

Appendices

Illustrated by Paris Simone Brower

Preface

A Parent's Guide to a Peaceful Home is critical for building a successful, peaceful home. It gives practical choices for how to teach our children responsibility, respect, discipline, and other character values.

It teaches the family how to relate to each other properly, which brings peace. You will be pleasantly surprised by how, if the tools and strategies are followed, the fussing between siblings and parents will cease. I know it is hard to believe, but it does work. You just have to do it. Everyone can learn how to turn toxic relationships into a wholesome family structure.

I live in a peaceful home, and we will have it no other way. I have had parents who diligently follow the strategies for a peaceful home. Their children's behavior changed at home and at school. The attitude change at school caused a domino effect with better self-concept, behavior, peer relations, grades, and happier teachers and parents.

As an example, a third grader was having issues at home and school. His teacher asked me to talk with him about his lack of attention, incomplete assignments and homework, and overall behavior. There were constant outbursts and disagreements with his peers.

I was walking down the hall when I saw a mother watching her son through the window. When I came back down the hall, she was still standing there. I noticed she was crying. I stopped and asked what was wrong and if I could help. She couldn't stop crying. She said, "My son." I told her I had to get back to my room, but I thought I could help. I made an appointment for her to see me after school.

Two days later, she, her husband, and John came to talk. I had set up an In School Suspension class to meet with parents and assist in helping them to work together to resolve such problems. I was able to help them work together, and John was able to work through his issues at home and at school.

I told his mother about affirmations and the importance of using them as she is training him. Using the words, "Teamwork makes the dream work," **TEAM**—**T**ogether **E**veryone **A**chieves **M**ore, helped to bring the family closer. (See Appendix V) They used it often to bring the family closer.

I saw the mother later, and she was all smiles. She said, "Thank you so much. You don't know how relieved we all are." She gave me a big hug. The family meeting was the solution that caused this family to work through John's issues, which brought peace to their home.

The bonus to this meeting was that John began to do his homework, get himself together in the mornings, and he didn't miss the bus. His mom didn't have to rush to work. Also, his class behavior and grades improved. I saw him at summer school. He was happy to tell me about his progress.

You will learn how to have family meetings and how important they are. Believe it or not, your children will get so involved in the family meetings that they will want and ask when they are going to have another one. I know this because I have class meetings when problems arise at school. They are on Fridays. Sometimes an emergency meeting is called when necessary.

Take a moment or two to visualize what you think a peaceful home should look like. Now, think about what your home looks like at this point. When this family meeting is done properly, your family will not want to go back because they will have become empowered with a healthy self-concept.

Towards Affective Development (TAD) is a program that assists youth in affecting lasting change from within. In TAD, children (tadpoles) mature into responsible adults. The program is presented at schools, PTAs, churches, conferences, and other organizations.

It took much praying, Bible reading, maturity, studying our children, meetings with parents, classes, training teachers, and reading other materials to find that when parents know what to do, they are grateful for the knowledge—especially when they see their children evolve into successful, responsible adults.

There are many new adults that I taught who are contributing to society in a positive manner. They and other likeminded young adults will take their places as the next generation of leaders, whether they become presidents, lawyers, doctors, ministers, teachers, architects, artists, entrepreneurs, or whatever else moves our society forward. These reasons are the motive behind this book.

"With God all things are possible" (Matt. 19:26, NIV).

Acknowledgments

I dedicate this book to a loving, living God who would not let me rest until I got the nerve to think about writing and then actually begin to write. I had a difficult time feeling like a writer—much less a skillful writer. Thank God for not giving up on me.

As I read the Bible daily, I kept running across a certain scripture: "My tongue is the pen of a skillful writer" (Ps. 45:1, NIV). It stayed on my mind constantly until God woke me one morning with the title of this book. I jumped out of bed to write it down so I would not forget it.

It was not difficult to understand why he gave me that title. I had conducted a pilot program in 2006, "The Peaceful Classroom," at Southampton Elementary School in Richmond, Virginia.

At Southampton, I became a permanent substitute and was able to implement my program Towards Affective Development (TAD), which helps students make changes within and become successful students in a peaceful classroom environment.

Thank you, God, for showing me the need for peace at school and at home—and for giving me the title and the ability to finally write it.

There were many times when I wanted to quit. When God gives you something, He will not let you quit. He gives me scriptures to confirm what He wants me to write.

"Now, finish the work so that your eagerness to do it may be matched by your completion of it, according to your means." (2 Cor. 8:11-12, NIV).

Thank you, God, for having faith in me to complete this book when I didn't have faith in myself.

I know now that this guide was not from me; it is for our children.

To my daughter, Kimberly J. Braxton-Brower, who is my best friend. I am thankful for your faith and insistence that I not give up. You know my heart like no one else besides God. You have lived with my untiring love for my students and know that my love for them goes deep to my core. Kim has seen me try to retire at least three times and just smiles when she sees me heading to schools as a permanent substitute with a special treat for the children that they must "earn". She was not surprised when I told her that God had given me a book to write.

I live with Kim, her husband, Eric Brower, Asia, and Paris. Our home is a peaceful one where love prevails. There are no arguments between the teenagers, husband, wife, or myself. I can write about a peaceful home because we live in one. It is possible. Thank you, Kim.

To Coach Eric Brower, my dear son-in-law who has finally seen me act on what he has been prompting me to do for years. He said, "Why not help many people, parents, and children learn how to raise disciplined children at home? Help them through workshops, conferences, and the PTA." Thank you for being such a great father. We need more people like you. Thanks, Coach. I finally did it!

To my loving and deceased parents, Mason and Virginia Powell, who were supportive in their love for me in all I attempted during their lifetimes. Their encouragement never stopped for their baby girl. Thank you, Mom and Dad. While you're not on this earth to see this monumental task that is now complete through God's continuous promptings, you watch from the portals of heaven. I want you to know there are five more books to come. I love you. Thanks for always believing in me. Your baby is so grateful that God chose me to do it. He never gave up on me.

To my granddaughters, Paris and Asia Brower. They are beautiful, intelligent, and disciplined. Both maintain B+ to A averages in school.

Paris is a six-foot-tall basketball player, and I am proud that she is capable of getting a basketball scholarship. She is receiving letters and calls from different colleges. I was surprised that Paris wants to be an Elementary Art teacher.

I am using this dedication to the girls as a springboard for parents. I want their example to inspire parents to start early (right after birth) to direct their children on the right path. However, it's not too late to pick up right where you are.

Thank you, girls, for assisting me with your technological skills. Paris illustrated the huge butterfly on the title page. She drew and photographed the picture for the appendix.

Asia has assisted in the initial typing and copying. Thank you. Asia will be completing college with a degree in civil engineering.

Sometimes when I asked them for help, I saw a quizzical look on their faces. I knew what they were thinking: *Nana, don't you know anything?*

To my siblings, the Powell's, (Scope) Mason, Marie, (Bunny) Clara and Irene:

Scope, you are there with a smile, encouragement, and your best advice. You boast about whatever I'm doing. There have been many things that I've ventured to do—haven't there?

To my sister, Marie Cain, who is so compassionate and still ready to share whenever you can: You have shown me a bigger life as I completed high school and permitted me to come to Cleveland to live with you. That is why I wrote this book. I learned to see the bigger picture of myself, so I decided to try fashion modeling in order to pay my college tuition as I entered John Carroll University. I quickly realized that fashion modeling was not for me! I was trying to look like you and be like you.

To Irene Wilkes, an awesome writer in your own right: You have walked beside me, assisted me, and given me a treasure of information when I asked, "What do I do next? How do I do that?" Irene, your never-give-up-until-you-win attitude has rubbed off on me. You know how hesitant I have been. However, here I am—an author.

To Clara Wilson (Bunny): You have a heart for studying the Word of God. You do it tirelessly and are ready to share that knowledge with all you come in contact with. Your love for the scriptures keeps you pushing and not giving up.

To the Wilsons: Anderson (Junior) and Barbara, you make me feel so special when I visit you. I always get a red-carpet reception, starting when I roll up to O' Taste N' See Restaurant and trying to decide how much and what to eat from the ribs, fish, and the best hamburger this side of heaven. I can't forget Barbara's banana pudding. Thanks again. These few words can't express my appreciation to you and your wonderful family. "You have done something right with all of your children; Larew; Keli, an Occupational Therapist-entrepreneur; Josiah, a Junior in computer engineering with a four year scholarship; and Rachael." Rachael is my other illustrator. Thank you for the beautiful cover picture. You worked hard to complete it and it is beautiful. Her plan is to enter college with an eye on the medical profession. I know Larew is looking down from heaven and saying, "Amen. I had the best parents. Now God has given you other wonderful children. I left you, but not in shame or disgrace. It was just my time to go. See you later." Aunt Pat is so very proud of you.

To my nephew, Dr. Wayne Oglesby (with your four or five degrees): Go man! Forgive me if I forget and call you "Shorty." After all, you are very tall now. I have not forgotten our long conversations about the one gift you said God had deposited in me. You informed me many years ago when I was floundering, knowing that there was a destiny for me—and I had the potential to make it happen. You said that thing was of major importance and that it was deep inside of me. You said, "You will know when it surfaces." You said that I would share it on a large scale. You believed it had something to do with children." You quoted Job 42:12-13, 16-17. The latter part of your life would be greater than the first. I will not live to be 140 years old like Job, but I believe I will live to see my grandchildren's children. They will certainly have an inheritance and a legacy. Thank you, Dr. Oglesby ("Shorty").

To my many nieces and nephews in different places: My wish for you is that the world is vast—and you make up a part of it. Take your piece of the puzzle and fit it in your place. You have a place. Keep looking, seeking, and praying. Most of all, listen to that wee small voice that keeps prompting you to move, go there, and stop! You will know if you listen. May God bless you all as you reach your potential.

Kenneth Jr. Braxton, my former husband and father of our daughter, is now deceased.

Kenneth was given a revolutionary concept for a computerized home security system in 1973 as he was attending his garden in Springfield, Illinois. He called it a gift from God. After six years of hard work, he was granted United States Patent #4,141,006 while we lived in Cedar Rapids, Iowa on February 20, 1979. Kenneth did not have the capital to manufacture and sell it, but we had inquiries from many countries.

His patent was for a computerized security device that could remotely zero in on a window or door under invasion, a building suddenly enveloped in flames, or the detection of gas fumes in buildings. Kenneth was elated with the system that could save lives.

In the *Cedar Rapids Gazette* on February 20, 1979, he said, "I had been reading about the thousands of people who lost their lives in fires, and I felt it was time for computers to be used in a practical way that would make sense to people and help solve this type of problem."

Kenneth, you had the heart to save lives. I wanted the world to know of your efforts even though you are not here to see it. You are a black man who made a contribution. You were one of the black inventors who got lost in the midst of history. We both wanted to help save families, but in different ways. Thank you.

To Pastor Randy and Pastor Cherie Gilbert of Faith Land Marks Ministries for their uncompromising teaching of the Word that propels us to reach our highest potential—and to make the most of ourselves because we represent the kingdom on this Earth. All should see the fruit that God deposited in us as we touch the lives of those around us so that they seek the God we serve and mankind's souls are saved.

Here is one of Pastor Randy's messages that I felt was "Just for me!"

> "Just for me" (Gen. 20-21).
>
> When the enemy hits you with everything all at the same time, he is trying to get you off course to cause you to let go of your destiny.
>
> God does not want you to forget who you are. Let your faith stay connected to your destiny.
>
> That thing that is in you is individual to you. Go toward your vision even while you are in the pit.
>
> Pastor Randy is speaking to you also. Let it be so: Amen (Gen. 50:20-21). You intended to harm me, but God intended it for my good to accomplish what is now being done, the saving of many lives. So, then, don't be afraid. I will provide for you and your children. Thanks to both of you.

I am grateful to Dr. Sheary D. Johnson, founder and president of the Ministry Connection, Inc., Better People, Inc., Women Empowerment Ministry, and Birthing a Vision, Inc., for her willingness to mentor me before the writing of this guide. You used your skills, wisdom, education, and godly vision throughout this and other ventures. You truly have become a partner, confidante, friend, and coworker when I needed help. Thank you for assisting me with the editing of this book. Your favorite scripture certainly does apply to our friendship: "Iron sharpeneth iron; so a man (woman) sharpeneth the countenance of his friends." (Prov. 27:17, NIV)

I sincerely thank the many ministers and pastors who have provided me with much enriched material to help enlighten my path.

To Eunice Kennedy-Shriver, founder of the Community of Caring Character Education Program from the Joseph P. Kennedy Foundation. Thank you for the impact this program has had on me and continues to have on our communities. I am also grateful for the confidence you placed in me to assist in developing, planning and implementing our school's Community of Caring Program.

To all the teachers and administrators who work tirelessly and unceasingly to teach and assist our children, our most precious resource. Thank you for the many, many hours of staying up until the middle of the night to grade papers, complete Report Cards (now online), write reports, make bulletin boards, and much more. Most of all, thank you for not giving up on our children. Thank you for your passion, which has given you longevity—even through the rough times. You stick it out because of your love for them.

It is widely known that teachers are not paid enough, especially when nearly everyone has had teachers that taught them to reach their destinies—yet we are almost at the bottom of the salary scale. That is truly sad. Many teachers have second and third jobs. This book is written for you. I want the world to get a glimpse at the dedication and hard work of most teachers because we love the children.

I can't speak for the administrators from the same perspective, but I know that their work must be triple what teachers do. Teachers work approximately 181 days a year. Administrators work approximately eleven to twelve months a year. A million thanks to you for a job well done. May God bless and keep you as you continue to work wonders.

Author's Note

As I researched the issues that face our children, I was astonished by the number of people who are making a difference in the lives of our children. I discuss some of them. There isn't enough paper to write about all of them. Kudos and blessings to all of you. You are giving back.

Many of these people are using their influence and dollars to reach millions of likeminded adults to partner with them in an effort to influence our youth in positive ways.

My plea to you is to get involved. Please research on the Internet to find out how you can be of the greatest assistance to your beloved children and God's beloved children.

There are resources in the back of this guide also that can help.

Introduction

After teaching thousands of children over the course of forty years, I was compelled to do my due diligence to the profession I so dearly love. I wanted to bring some light from "the horse's mouth."

My experiences in classrooms in four states all had a common thread. All children—from babes to teenagers—respond to love, kindness, and compassion. They don't care how much you know until they know how much you care. This includes all adults they come in contact with.

I realize that many older youths and adults have used this knowledge to lure and entrap children and teenagers into doing lewd things. They destroy their dignity and take away their wholesomeness, which lowers their self-esteem. This leaves them in a vulnerable state.

Many have also lost their lives because of their need for relationships. Children cannot decipher true love and compassion from the shrewdness of the perpetrators. How can they? Many adults have also fallen because of the shrewdness of people.

I acknowledge the contribution of Eunice Kennedy-Shriver, founder of the Community of Caring Character Education Program from the Joseph P. Kennedy Foundation to schools in the United States and, in particular, Reid Elementary in Richmond, Virginia. The inspiration for this book came from my association with Mrs. Eunice Kennedy-Shriver and the Community of Caring.

It takes a whole village to raise a child—this is what Mrs. Shriver endeavored to do. For twenty-five years, she had been devoted to serving children, families, and communities around the United States. She said, "Today we must make the foundation of our community and our national life the virtues of caring: caring for our children, caring for our families, for strangers, and always caring for persons with mental retardation."

I heard these words at my first Community of Caring Conference in Kansas City, Missouri, in July 1994. I had the pleasure to meet Mrs.

Kennedy-Shriver there; it was not difficult to see and feel her love for children and their parents. There were hundreds of us at the annual conference. It was our responsibility to take Community of Caring back to our schools and communities for implementation. The teachers who were there were facilitators for their schools. Our function was to assist in carrying out the Community of Caring Character Education Program.

There were three of us from Reid Elementary in Richmond. Linda Wallace, Edward Green, and I assisted our school in implementing this program successfully for five years.

In our first circle meeting, Mrs. Kennedy-Shriver discussed her program with us. She asked Linda and me a question and wrote our names on a sheet of paper.

It wasn't long after that meeting that we were asked to come to Washington to serve on a national committee to develop *How to Create a Community Caring Elementary Guide*. The guide consisted of values and ethics based on the program. It outlined the content for the comprehensive curriculum for elementary schools throughout the nation. The teachers were responsible for lesson plans in reading, language arts, math, social studies, science and motivation to foster self-esteem and reinforce values. We were required to incorporate character values into each of our lesson plans for the guide.

Patricia Braxton

• Patricia Braxton and Linda Wallace, teachers at G. H. Reid Elementary School, have been selected to serve on a national committee responsible for developing an elementary school curriculum guide for the values and ethics-based Community of Caring program.
    The two, who serve as Reid's facilitators for the program, met with educators from across the country in Washington, D.C. to outline the content for what will eventually become a comprehensive curriculum guide for elementary schools throughout the nation.

Linda Wallace

News Letter: The School Bell Volume 30 No. 2   1994

The Richmond City Public Schools publish news of various accomplishments of their teachers and staff. The information therein reports Linda Wallace and myself after having been selected to serve on a national committee for the Community of Caring in 1994.

Following the completion of the guide, two schools were chosen to participate in Community of Caring's first video. The video, *Five Little Words That Can Change Your Life,* was filmed at G. H. Reid Elementary School in Richmond, Virginia, and at a high school in Utah. The five little words are the character Core Values: Respect, Responsibility, Caring, Trust and Family. Linda's class was featured as she demonstrated how to incorporate the core values in the existing adopted basal reading textbooks. Kathy Flickenger, a kindergarten teacher, was also featured in the video. Our school counselor, Ed Green, discussed the overall concept of character values and how they shaped our school environment. I was included in the credits for my participation. The video demonstrated how the Community of Caring program can adapt itself to the school district's curriculum, interspersing the core values in every aspect of the function of the schools.

All faculty and staff members participated in the program. The Community of Caring fits itself under the school's umbrella and enhances it. A number of teachers were selected to become National Trainer of Trainers. We collaborated to write *The Community of Caring Trainer's Manual.* Edward Green, our counselor, and I were among those chosen. The program was developed to provide schools with ideas, materials, training, support, and resources to encourage thoughtful discussion and continuous reinforcement of the five core values among students, parents, teachers, community leaders, administrators, and other personnel who touch children's lives. Based on its previous successes with adolescents, the scope of program was expanded to include all children in grades K-12.

The Community of Caring Program, a product of the Joseph P. Kennedy Jr. Foundation, was founded in 1982 for the primary purpose of reducing the risks of adolescent pregnancy and mental retardation. The medical profession indicates that babies born to teenage mothers are at increased risk for mental retardation.

Results obtained by the original Community of Caring were excellent—not only in enhancing other aspects of adolescents but in social and emotional development as well (*Community of Caring Manual Draft #1*, p. 2, Appendix).

Mrs. Kennedy-Shriver created the Special Olympics as a result of the large number of babies born with mental retardation and intellectual challenges. Retardation can be caused by low birth weight due to poor nutrition, lack of prenatal care, or drug use during pregnancy. Mrs. Shriver used athletics to change the lives of children.

Today, more than three million Olympians train year-round in all fifty states and 181 countries. They have shown they are capable—even though some of them were once locked up in institutions. Medical treatment has changed for people with intellectual disabilities as a result of Mrs. Shriver's vision. Attitudes, minds, and laws have also changed to include them on every level (www.eunicekennedyshriver.org).

I include this information in reference to Special Olympics to further cite her meritorious actions and dedication to our children, parents, and community in our school systems world-wide.

The Community of Caring Program remained at G. H. Reid Elementary from 1994 until 1999. It was extremely successful. During one of her visits to Reid, Mrs. Shriver was amazed by the progress we had made by incorporating the program into the school district's existing curriculum. She visited classrooms, talked, and interacted with students. She was excited to see our progress. At the end of the day, we surprised her with students who we showcased in musical activities.

She was most pleased by a program from our now deceased music teacher, Joan Richardson. The "World Ensemble" had at least 100 students from Reid and some former students who remained in the group. They were in middle and high school. Some of them were dancers, choir members, and drummers.

While sitting beside her, she got "in the beat" of the African drummers and dance troupes. She had a huge grin on her face. She said, "I am overwhelmed at the talent of these young students and their teacher."

Although the program was during the day, many parents supported Mrs. Richardson and the school and were included in the film.

Mrs. Shriver said, "I love the warm feeling this school has. You feel it when you enter the building."

During the fifth year of Community of Caring at Reid, Mr. Kite, a fifth-grade teacher, went on to be a principal at Albert High Middle School. He is now with University of Virginia's Annual Yearly Progress (AYP) Program. I was teaching fourth grade.

Mr. Kite said, "Ms. Braxton, you won't believe the class I have this year! I have never had a class like this! They are wonderful! They are passing all the tests! They are well behaved and are so kind to each other. They respect each other and are very responsible."

We stopped, looked at each other, and said, "The Community of Caring."

We both laughed. The students had been in kindergarten five years prior—when the Community of Caring came to Reid. The fifth graders had been mentors for the kindergarteners. Each teacher permitted the students to exchange once a week so that all the fifth graders were assisting. There were times when the kindergartners went up to fifth grade and sat beside their mentor as the teacher was teaching.

Many students were able to go read to them in the morning or afternoon. The students who went through those five years had similar successes.

At a national conference in Salt Lake City, I was preparing to give my presentation when Mrs. Shriver motioned for me to come to her.

She said, "We have not been including enough information about the family. Would you please include the family in your presentation?"

I had not prepared any mention of the family in my presentation—and I was the first presenter. I can't remember how long I stood in bewilderment, but I managed to say, "Yes. I will."

Who could say "no" to her? I think I forgot to be scared. I prayed, "Lord, help me do this." I did what she asked, and she thanked me.

She said, "I am pleased. From now on, the family will be much more of an integral part of our conferences."

> This program works. Independently compiled statistics show that in Community of Caring Schools, teenage pregnancy has dramatically reduced. Drugs and alcohol are on the decline. Student attendance, and grade-point averages are up.
>
> For example, from Armstrong High School in Richmond, Virginia, the principal wrote, "All five years of being a Community of Caring school, the teenage pregnancy rate has been reduced 60 percent, the drop-out rate has gone down and most importantly, Armstrong has the fewest number of student referral violations of the Student Standard of Conduct for each of the last five years." *The Evening Sun,* "A program that teaches teen-agers to care." (July 3, 1995, Bill Moyers PBS Report on Violence in America)

How about that! Why wouldn't schools support a program such as this? There are other programs, however I can only discuss the one I know that has had positive results.

If your school or system is looking for a character education program that has a proven record for success, I suggest the Community of Caring Education Program. Community of Caring has been adopted by almost 1,400 schools and is serving over 1,000,000 students in forty-six states.

I am proud to announce that five elementary schools in Richmond have adopted Community of Caring: Bellevue Elementary School, Chimborazo Elementary School, Fairfield Court Elementary School, George Mason Elementary School, and Woodville Elementary School. Watch out! Children are blossoming!

Thanks, Mrs. Kennedy-Shriver. I speak for the millions of students you have touched through your vision. Your legacy will live on through generations.

I dedicate this guide to the thousands of children and young adults I have taught. To all children, this guide is specifically for you. Many of us are working on plans to create a better atmosphere in which to live.

It is my desire and dream that all who love our children will read this guide in its entirety and use the tools and strategies to transform your homes into a place where our children are nurtured, valued, and empowered to live a life before your children that perpetuates the very principal that love does change things and love never fails (1 Cor. 13:16).

To all children and youth, you have the potential to be what you desire. "Nothing is impossible to you." God said, "With man this is impossible but with God all things are possible" (Matt. 10:27). Be, Do, Have . . .

Get that desire deep down inside of you. Say it, see it, and do it. Remember these words in that order. In your mind, see yourself being it, doing it, and then you can have it. You will see these words a few times as you read.

See yourself as the Lord sees you. You will be the head and not the tail if you follow His commands. He also says you will be on top and never on the bottom (Deut. 28:13).

Let's show what you're made of! I love you all and thank you for making this world a better place to live.

To the ones who are now in elementary, middle and high school, you already know, it's impossible to name you all. Think of what a humongous book that would be!

This guide is written from my heart especially with all of you in mind, in order that you might stretch to reach your potential.

I am so very proud of my former students, the Adrienne's, Destiny's, Gabriel's and Johnny's who are now successful. You are engineers, doctors, teachers, preachers, authors, entrepreneurs, lawyers, business owners, entertainers, professors, dentists, and the ones who are still in college, I honor you for your future pursuits and contributions to society. It is important that you don't exclude God as you continue through life. I saw it in you—even in elementary school. It is up to you to make sure you carve out a legacy for your children's children.

To the ones who have not reached your destiny, it's not too late. Look back at what you love, and are good at. Ask God to guide you as you follow his instructions. "Go confidently in the direction of your dreams." (Henry David Thoreau)

The Peaceful Home

Not one person, mother, or family on God's green earth wants their offspring not to develop into well disciplined, successful human beings, but some parents really do not know what to do and how to make it work. I want to make an apology here. I thought that some parents didn't care because of the lack of participation in helping their children with homework and working to resolve discipline issues at school. If they knew better, they would do better. Maya Angelou said that if people know better, they will do better. That is worth repeating. All parents and people in general want a peaceful home—and now it is possible.

I believe that we can help change the face of many families with this guide. I know it is a tall order and can seem impossible, but nothing will be impossible for you with God (Matt. 19:20, NIV).

Repeat "I'm possible" over and over again and believe it because God said it! You will notice that with the insertion of an apostrophe, impossible becomes "I'm possible."

Some homes where chaos reigns will be changed into large family gatherings that will spill over into the neighborhoods. This will be discussed in the chapter on family meetings.

We must, through the hand of God, turn what has become a nightmare in too many cities into something wonderful for our children. However, we must work together as a TEAM (Together Each Achieves More) because teamwork makes the dream work. This is an achievable, simple, easy-to-follow, inexpensive solution. The most you will spend will be the cost of this book plus a few dollar store items, and it won't hurt a bit. In fact, your children will love working as a team to have and keep this new wonderful, peaceful home that all have been working so hard to achieve.

The real key behind this is a change from within by all participants. It begins with Mom (the adults) being the first to surprise her children.

Mom begins the process. Romans 12:2 says, "Do not be conformed by this world, but be transformed by the renewal of your mind."

Webster's Dictionary says transform means to change markedly in form or appearance, to change the nature, function of, convert, or be converted. This is what TAD means.

It is possible to convert what was once a dysfunctional home into a functional one by enforcing and reinforcing by example what you want your home to look like. A house where love, compassion, respect, and other virtues are taught by example and reinforced will produce a lasting, peaceful home. No adult reading this will say, "I don't want that!"

Since some things previously said will be repeated for emphasis, don't say, "Why does she keep repeating the same thing?" That's what teachers do. I have learned as a teacher that it takes twenty to thirty times to get something to stick in our brains. If you want your children to retain their spelling words and their math facts, try this strategy.

As you read, you are probably wondering what's up with all of these butterflies on all of the pages. They are to remind you of the complete change, conversion, and transformation forthcoming from all family participants. Butterflies are the logo for TAD.

Home before School

Part I: Let's Begin at the Beginning

It all begins with the parent. To successfully ensure a peaceful home, you begin the process. After all, parents are children's first teachers. Over a period of time, you have formed a relationship with your children. Whether it has been positive or negative, they have seen your reactions to different situations and have programmed these actions and reactions in their computers (their brains). They remember your exact words and sometimes mouth them to each other behind your back. They can even act them out.

How do I know? I know because I did it—and so did you! We were smart enough not to let our parents see us. Right? I am asking you to change your way of doing some things for the benefit of building a peaceful home. Actually, you will begin using a number of strategies to surprise them. Soon everyone will be so curious that they will be asking each other, "What's happening?" Everyone will like the cat and mouse game and the warm, fuzzy feeling that develops. These changes can benefit the family for a lifetime.

You want your children to emulate the positive things they see you do. When children are asked who their heroes or idols are, they normally give the names of sports stars, hip-hop singers, or other celebrities. I have seldom heard them name a mom, dad, or other family member. That is unfortunate. Our children deserve better than that. I hope I have built a significant case to warrant a house change that has to begin with you. Do not worry; it will not hurt. You will be glad you did! Do not reveal the reason for this change. Just continue to keep them in suspense. This will cause them—and you—to form a new relationship without pushing it. It will just happen. You will let them know why you have made changes at a later date.

In order to get your children to buy into the new version of the transformed parent, you will need to stick to the changes. They must see a new, different attitude and behavior around the house and other places over a period of time. A month is sufficient. Romans 12:2 says, "Do not be conformed to this world, but be transformed by the renewing of your mind." That means you are capable of doing things a new way.

I will come back to how you will be transformed. Not only will your children come to love the new you, but also you will love the newly changed you. I'm taking this side road in order for you to see that this guide did not happen overnight. It didn't happen without commitment; therefore, you will not have a peaceful home without commitment.

It is important for me to express how a Goethe's Couplet and some corresponding Scriptures impacted my life. They are the reasons you are reading this guide.

Goethe's Couplet

> Are you in earnest.
> Seize the moment.
> Whatever you can do or dream, you can do, begin it.
> Boldness has genius, magic, and power in it.
> Only energize and the mind goes heated.
> Begin and then the work will be completed.
> The moment one definitely commits oneself,
> Providence moves in.
> God is Providence.
> All sorts of things occur which would never have occurred.
> A whole stream of events issues from that decision,
> Raising in one's favor all manner of unforeseen incidents
> And meetings and material assistance,
> Who no man could have dreamt would come his way.

I became committed to not let anything keep me from completing this guide. Scripture confirmed my inner feeling and the necessity not to give up. "Now finish the work, so that your eager willingness to do it may be matched by your completion of it according to your means" (2 Cor. 8:11, NIV) "Whatever you have in your mind do it, for God is with you" (1 Cor. 17:2, NIV). These are the words Nathan spoke to David. I thought if these words were good enough for David, they are good enough for me!

Goethe's couplet and the scriptures so penetrated my soul and changed the way I began to think about myself and what I was capable of doing. There were plenty obstacles that tried to prevent me from finishing this book. Fear was the greatest obstacle. *Who do you think you are? What makes you think you can write a book that others will read?*

Using time wisely was another obstacle I had to overcome because plenty of issues cropped up that stopped me for periods of time and prevented me from writing. I had to make time to write even when I was tired, sleepy, or doubtful.

When obstacles kept rearing their ugly heads, I had to fight over and over and over again to remain committed.

My first discovery of Goethe's couplet occurred at our Faith Landmarks Bible Institute graduation in June 2006. Bishop Joseph Garlington was our graduation speaker. He recited it so eloquently and electrifyingly as he commended the graduates for their commitment to complete the classes. He admonished them to remain committed to do the work for the Lord for which they had started.

As he recited it, I wrote it down quickly with tears in my eyes. It struck a chord in my spirit that I never forgot. I folded it up and put it in my wallet. It became dirty and grungy as I reread it over the next four years. I committed it to memory over the period of time.

About three years later, I was leafing through the September 2006 issue of *O Magazine* and saw these words. "Once you decide what you want, you make a commitment to that decision." I knew without reading the article that it was Goethe's couplet. It was in the section "What I Know for Sure."

The article was about a young mother who couldn't get her three-year-old son to go to bed without hours of trauma and drama. An expert on these matters, Dr. Stanley Turecki, watched a tape of the problem. He said, "Nothing happens until you decide."

When the mother decided, made up her mind, and committed herself, her son finally went to sleep in his own bed.

Oprah noted that the advice applied to many other aspects of life. "Relationships, career moves, weight issues—everything depends on your decisions."

The premise behind *A Parent's Guide to a Peaceful Home* is building positive relationships within the family. First, the parent needs to commit to building that home. No commitment, no peaceful home.

The more I recited the couplet, the more excited and committed I became. Finally, I started conducting PTA meetings, conferences, and workshops at schools and churches on The Peaceful Home. I discussed and recited Goethe's couplet and told how I encountered this rare jewel in the first place.

Thanks to Maxine Wyche, office assistant at Southampton Elementary in Richmond, who typed the couplet in cursive font and put it on beautiful flowered paper. It is suitable for framing. I pass it out at these meetings. It has been my hope that many others would read it and become committed to building a peaceful home.

I couldn't ask you to read Goethe's couplet without explaining how it has impacted me, the young mother, Oprah, and many others. I expect more people will read the scriptures and the couplet and commit themselves to whatever seems so difficult.

Envision your future home environment. Write your vision in a journal for future reference and discussions with your children. You will be able to see what is and what was. This exercise will further validate your commitment to a positive atmosphere. Throughout this book, you will be asked to go first in various exercises. As parents, we are teaching all the time whether we realize it or not. They are watching us.

A disciplined parent will gain the respect of their children. When you change your behaviors, they will see their parents disciplining themselves in order to begin the change toward a peaceful home. Remember you are not to tell them what you have been doing. In other words, you will begin this process by doing and being rather than talking.

They will expect to see this behavior continue. Guess what they are thinking? *I'm also going to be expected to act differently.* They will be easier to discipline, and respect will follow.

"Discipline your son for in them there is hope" (Prov. 19:18).

"An undisciplined parent breeds undisciplined children. An undisciplined child has no hope." This embodies the true reason for this book. I know what I am asking is not impossible to do. Parents are fierce when it comes to the children. They will lift a car if they have to! It has been documented. I am not asking for anything close to that. I am asking you to commit yourself to building a peaceful home where all will flourish, fulfill their God-given potential, and become a valuable resource to society. I know I am not asking too much. Won't you agree?

I am returning from my side road trip. I'll bet you thought I forgot. Transformation begins.

Here are two common scenarios where parents might blow up. After these examples, you will come up with your own positive solutions. Okay. Here we go.

Scenario 1

Your child has just broken another plate, and you are down to a very few. You are the adult, so let's act like it. Okay! Think before you speak! Think about the screaming and hollering that may normally follow this incident. You are the adult, and you can handle it appropriately.

Say, "I know it was an accident. Let me clean it up because I don't want you to get cut. Please get the broom, dustpan, and some plastic bags." Before, you would probably have gotten it up but fussed the whole time as you were sweeping it up. "It's okay. Plates are not nearly as important as you are. Plates can be replaced but not you. I'm so glad you didn't get hurt."

It is important not to show anger at this time. Remember, they are playing over in their heads what normally happens—and they know what you will say and do. Just think about the impact that it will have on the child. You are on your way to a peaceful home. The children will be holding their breath, wondering what will happen next. With a sigh of relief, they will begin to smile inside.

You have heard these words before—haven't you? Children resemble their parents in more ways than appearance. They are a reflection of what they see and hear primarily at home. Some of what they have seen and heard was positive or negative, and it plays out in their actions with their siblings, peers, and adults. These positive or negative behaviors go on to play an important role at school, church, and in the community. If the behavior is positive, they are most likely to have a well-rounded school experience.

As a seasoned teacher, I have observed that when a student is well-rounded, they have a healthy self-concept. They are more likely to have good conduct and are able to focus better on instructions. They are not easily distracted. Therefore, it stands to reason that they will retain what is taught. The added reward is good or great grades. Being on the Honor Roll is an excellent booster of self-confidence.

On the other hand, if children are coming to school after negative, frustrating situations at home, the opposite situations will occur. These children will most likely have a poor self-concept, which will bring about poor citizenship. This will keep them from following directions and focusing during instruction, causing lower grades.

Students who continually make poor grades tend to act inappropriately by disrupting their peers and the teacher, which shortens the teaching time. Everyone is affected. There are no rewards, and a lack of self-confidence occurs. The domino effect started with a poor self-concept.

I can safely say that no parent or guardian will wish these circumstances on their own children. On the other hand, these situations will continue unless the caregiver takes appropriate steps to correct these behaviors.

Don't worry. I didn't forget about the plate incident. This story was necessary to show the importance of children coming from a disciplined, peaceful home with the parent serving as the first teacher. It is for the love of children that we do what we do. In this scenario, children see the parents voluntarily disciplining themselves. At this point, it will not be difficult to expect respect and discipline from them; after all, they saw you do it.

Scenario 2

What if the child deliberately threw the plate? You have probably had similar episodes where you lost it and said things you later regretted. Surprisingly, your reaction should not be one of anger, but let them see the caring, disciplined adult show up.

Let them see you being thoughtful. Bite your lip and say, "I know you are angry; otherwise, you would not have thrown that plate. What would have happened if the plate had hit me or your brother or sister—and we were severely cut? I know you would not want that." Look the child straight in the eye. Look for any sign of remorse. Nine times out of ten, you will see it. You will probably see some alligator tears. Get close to the child and pat them on the shoulder, and say, "We will discuss this later, but now I need you to get the broom, the dustpan, and some plastic bags. I will get it up because I don't want you to get cut."

I don't think you will see any more flying saucers because all the siblings will have seen everything! Now you have their attention! They will look at each other and wonder what is happening? They will like it!

Look at the perpetrator and calmly say, "Why don't you go to your room and think about what you did. Write what you did and why? I also need you to write what you should have done and what you will do the next time you get angry." (Give them a copy of the Think Sheet located in the appendix.)

This exercise should take at least half of an hour. Let me tell you from the horse's mouth—they hate this exercise! They do not like to sit and think about what to write. I have found this exercise alone will cause them to think twice before doing something else negative.

This is a good time to have a mini-meeting. When the child comes back with the Think Sheet, say, "You know this behavior will cost you something. Let me hear what you suggest should happen?" Listen and come up with an appropriate punishment. Sometimes their suggestions are worse than what you would have suggested.

If you have little ones who cannot read, have a short discussion with them. Ask them to think about what they did. Ask them what they should have done. Remember, you are not fussing with them. Ask them what they will do the next time. They are thinking and taking ownership of their behavior.

If they are too little to write, have a predetermined place for them to sit. Tell them why they must sit there—and how long. It should not be longer than fifteen minutes.

You probably will have to be committed and determined to redirect them when they move or have a fit. You must wear them out with your determination that they sit and stay in that spot for a while.

Here is another strategy I want you to remember as you guide your children and yourself. It is the use of these three little words which must be used in the order given: Be. Do. Have.

Here are the strategies and steps to follow that will gain their respect and help you become more disciplined. First, they saw you acting differently. They watched you change your language and attitude during the broken plate incident.

Secondly, they observed you doing and saying positive things. You swept up the broken plate so they would not get cut. That showed them love and compassion.

Thirdly, you gain their respect. They have changed their behavior, and you have their attention.

You will have a peaceful home if you continue these positive actions. You were not aware that you automatically followed these three little words in order until I pointed them out. I believe you will remember them—not only for yourself—while interacting with your children in every aspect.

Be different from the way you used to be. Do things differently than you did before. Now, you have what you all want—a peaceful home where you all can be successful.

It is possible for your children to have success at school in all areas if you focus your attention on each of them through the meetings. Being attentive lets them know you care. They will follow your lead and be attentive to each other, their chores, their homework, and their study habits. This will be discussed more in the meeting section.

Think about how these incidents have impacted your children. You know your children—and they know you. Think about the incidents that have occurred over the years. You all know how you have reacted whether negatively or positively.

Once they have seen the new disciplined you, they will love it! They are anticipating what the future holds. You will continue to react in a positive manner when incidents occur.

What if you revert back? Call a meeting, sit them down, and fess up like a lady, a loving mother. Apologize for your actions. Tell them that Mama makes mistakes just like you do. Milk this for all it's worth. Ask for forgiveness. They will learn to apologize and ask for forgiveness when they make mistakes. If you want them to make changes, you must go first.

It is not hard to do this in my classrooms. If I accuse the wrong child of talking, I apologize. I explain that I am human and make mistakes just as they do. I have a day of asking forgiveness and apologies.

Because of your actions and reactions, they will feel valued deep inside. They will want this to continue. They will discuss and tell all who will listen about their "new mom." These actions will cause them to have the best sleep of their lives because they have seen you voluntarily discipline yourself. It will not be difficult to expect respect from them because they saw you respect them first. You will become the one they respect and love most—not their idol. How cool is that?

You will cause a domino effect in your home. They will learn to respect their siblings at home, their peers at school, peers and people in general, at church, their community at large, and the world in which they live.

I have a perfect example of young parents who actually began to think about appropriate names for their children before their birth. They envisioned who they wanted their children to become. They chose unusual names for them. I can dare to say they are the only children with those names. The oldest, Excellence, is now thirteen. He has been in private school since Montessori. Of course, Excellence is living up to his name. He is excelling in all subjects, sports, and has received numerous awards. Excellence is an avid reader and can read a 1,500-page book in a few days. His sister, Triumph, is a second grader. She is "triumphing" in school, earning awards, and is also an avid reader. Both have excellent citizenship. Their futures look very promising. Their parents are God-fearing with a no-nonsense attitude about training and disciplining the children. God has blessed them in their efforts.

The Perry's prepared them for school at home. Since 95 percent of a child's brain is formed by four or five, that is the time most training and discipline should be done. We do them a disservice when we send them to school unprepared. They start out lost, and it is very difficult to bridge that gap. They can end up lost.

Since the Bible, people have named their offspring what they were inspired to call them—and they became what they were called. Call them inappropriate names, and they will live up to what you call them. "As a man thinketh in his heart, so is he" (Prov. 23:7, NIV). This is not only true for the Perry children; it is true for all of us. Let's think more highly about our children. Tell them through your words, hugs, and kisses.

There is a reason I know so much about the Perry's. Mr. Perry is my second cousin. They call me Auntie Nana because they say I act like an Aunt and I am a Nana (grandmother).

Home before School

Part II: Wise Parents

Throughout this guide, I mention meetings because they are paramount to the success of a peaceful home.

While I was writing about meetings, I was reminded of my parents (God rest their souls) and how they disciplined us as children. When my siblings (Scope/Mason, Marie, Bunny/Clara, Irene, and I get together, we often reflect on them and the whippings with laughter. Apparently their method of correction left no bitterness in our hearts.

We didn't have any meetings. There was not a discussion when we were found guilty. Sometimes we were met at the door with a switch. No talking was necessary. Talk would often come later. The irony of this is that we had to go get our own switches! We all knew what size switch to get! As I'm writing this, I am smiling as memories play in living color.

Once in a blue moon, Mom would talk to us about the situations and our misdeeds. None of us wanted a "talking to." We preferred the spanking because a talking to lasted too long! We would rather have the spanking because it was over in a minute or two, and we wanted to get back to playing. Then she would add, "It hurts me more than it hurts you to have to 'spank' or 'whip' you." We didn't dare say anything, because what we were thinking would have caused more of the same.

Our parents were wise in raising us. They used the spare-the-rod-and-spoil-the-child rule (Prov. 13:24, NIV).

They said, "You can't pull the wool over my eyes." That meant we couldn't fool them. They knew what each of their five children were capable of doing. They could pinpoint each one of our wrongdoings from experience. We couldn't back out of anything because we were guilty 99.9 percent of the time.

To show you the God-given wisdom of a mother who went to the eleventh grade and raised five children, I have selected one of my stories.

I was about five or six years old when my mom let me go to the store a "little way" up the street. I went to get myself an orange which cost a nickel. When I went to the store, it was crowded. I went to the counter to pay for it. There were many tall people in front of me. I waited a little while, turned around, and went home with the orange and the nickel. As I was getting ready to eat the orange, I put the nickel on the table.

Mom said, "Pat, why do you still have the nickel and the orange?"

I tried to explain my way out of it. Mom was not at all interested in my explanation! I had just "stolen" an orange, and that was the end of my talking!

She said, "Take that orange back to the store and explain very loudly to Mr. Johnson that you stole his orange! I will ask him how you confessed and if you told him you were sorry and would never do that again?"

I still remember vividly how embarrassed I was! *If stealing is this bad, I won't ever do that again!* My face had shame all over it, and tears were running down my face. It seemed like a thousand people were in that store peering at me! All I could see were eyes! That was it! I knew stealing was nothing I wanted to ever do again in my life!

Parents, there is a reason I told this story. Over the years, many of my students thought it was okay to pick up and keep whatever lay in their view—pencils, money, or lunches. Sometimes they would say, "My mom told me if a pencil is on the floor, I could keep it." Parents, this is condoning stealing. I would say, "If your mother didn't buy it, it's not yours."

I had to teach them that stealing can get you in big trouble when you are older. That is a habit you don't want to cultivate. This should not be a part of the teacher's job. It's yours. Many of our kids and adults are in jail or dead because they started stealing early and were not corrected at home.

When we showed any disrespect during the discipline as teenagers, our parents said, "I brought you in this world, and I'll take you out. Don't even think it! I'll knock you into the middle of next week!" We knew it was impossible, but the thoughts behind those words stopped us in our tracks!

Our parents did not try to hide our misdeeds and all of our family members and adults knew. They would let us know they knew and promised a spanking. They sometimes actually gave us another spanking "for good measure."

During those times, the whole village was raising us. We were admonished that we had to respect all adult people—not just our aunts and uncles. Color made no difference.

We had to be on our P's and Q's wherever we went. None of us went to jail. As a matter of fact, it was taboo to be sent to the Principal's Office.

Stratton High School in Beckley, West Virginia, had a "Black Book" that was reserved for those who broke school rules. No one wanted to go to the Principal's Office for fear of your name being put in the Black Book. None of us got our names in that book!

There was a healthy respect for our school, our teachers, and all who worked at the school. We had dynamic teachers at our segregated school.

Many of us went on to be doctors, lawyers, teachers and professors, business owners. Some held city and state offices. There was at least one inventor. I guess I should not leave out authors.

As a veteran teacher, I have seen a certain scenario play out so many times. A mother brings her son or daughter to the new school. Many times, it's close to the middle of the school year. The secretary would bring the parent and the fifth grader to my classroom and introduce them. After the introduction, I would ask the children about their experiences at their previous schools.

I said, "Do you like school?"

"Yes."

"How was your behavior at that school?"

"Good." Mom nodded her head and said, "Yes. There were no problems."

"What kind of grades did you make?"

"Oh, I made all A's and B's."

Mom said, "Yes, my child was on the Honor and or Scholar Roll ever since being in school."

Many times, continued disobedience resulted in the parent moving the child thinking a change of location might change the child's behavior.

The disruptive behavior started immediately after the parent left.

Upon meeting with mom, I said, "What changes in behavior have occurred between the time when you took your child out of the previous school and now? Why would the child automatically make the behavior adjustment on his/her own without correction on your part?"

Parents and children know that nothing different is expected at the new school. The child can continue the same behavior. On the very first day, the child has problems that will continue throughout their scholastic career. Many times, they hate school and can't wait to drop out physically because they have already dropped out mentally.

If you want something different to happen with your children, you will have to do something different. You must discuss what is and is not going to happen at the new school—and follow through. Call the teacher that first evening to see how the day went and call many more times so your child will get a clue that you no longer will tolerate negative behavior!

I have a method of correction that almost always works. I will discuss that in a later chapter. I do not have them get their own switch.

The disruptive behavior is most often the reason for below grade-level scores. If they are constantly off-task, not following directions or listening, they do more than keep themselves from learning. They make it difficult for their classmates to learn and especially difficult for the teacher to teach.

I hope that you will see that removing a disobedient child from a school will not make a difference in behavior or in academic progress.

Please don't let your child hear you say something that is untrue. Make sure you are being honest. You are their first teacher. What are you teaching them? Do not condone negative behavior. Are you teaching honesty or dishonesty?

Heads up! Parents, your child's records arrived at school before the child does. The report card shows academic results and social behavior for the number of years your child has been in school.

Please use wisdom to correct your children and set boundaries that you have discussed with them during your family meetings. If boundaries are not set at home, many of our children end up in places that cause heartbreak and heartache that lasts a lifetime.

Parents and caregivers, you have so many more opportunities than our parents did. They had the wisdom of God to guide them, which made the difference. We also had a close-knit community or village where everybody knew each other and parents watched out after each others' children.

You have God but not necessarily your immediate neighborhood to assist. Your village may be a larger group of mentors. I see a proliferation of them from almost all states, willing and ready to help.

God is directing this huge effort. Take advantage of the opportunities that come your way. Ask and it shall be given unto you. Seek and you shall find. Knock and the door will be opened to you (Matt. 4:7-11, NIV).

Use your computers to find them. Mentors in every city and state are waiting to help children, young adults, and parents. There are resources in the appendix for your use.

President Obama says, "Be the change you seek." You must show interest in your children and do whatever is necessary to raise up your children in the way they should go and when they are old they will not depart from it? (Prov. 22:6, NIV). They will emulate the positive things you have taught them or the negative things you have taught them.

In one of the many commencement addresses made by President Obama, I hurriedly wrote down what I heard. The speech was exactly what this whole guide is about—family support at home.

"No party or policy can take the place of parents. Responsibility begins at home with parents. Go to the PTA meetings. Help with homework. Turn off the TV and video games. This is an American issue—not a republican or democratic issue.

It is my desire to help you become wise parents. "A wise man (woman) has great power and a man (woman) of knowledge increases strength for waging war (against anything that comes to dismantle the family)" (Prov. 24:5-6, NIV).

You need guidance and many advisors for victory. Avail yourself of the resources out there because there are many mentors and advisors whose only goal is to help families and children.

Through my research, many of them are black men. Many work in sports, movies, entertainment, or politics. There are pastors, educators, doctors, lawyers, and more. It has been said too many times that black men are only interested in their own ventures. From my research, many are not asking families for monetary assistance. They have grants, foundations and sponsors that use their names for expanding a mission or passion. Black, Caucasian, Asian, Indian, and Hispanic women have done—and are doing—outstanding things for our children that are just as noteworthy. Many women are holding down two jobs—one at home—and a career. Some have started schools or foundations and gotten grants to help children.

We cannot top Oprah and Michelle Obama, but we can all do as much as we can—with all that we can—as often as we can. Parents, your most crucial job starts in your home.

There is a cry from everywhere to save our children.

Home before School

Part III: Be, Do, Have

Parents, of all of the guidance I have proposed in this book, this piece is most crucial. An infinite number of families have been destroyed in too many ways to enumerate for making wrong choices. You have your own story. If I could be your Mama or Nana in this book, I would be most rewarded. Please don't take this advice lightly. You didn't have to spend an arm and a leg to receive it.

Be very careful, from this point on, with whom you associate. Your future and your children's futures depend on it. God will send you the proper people. Ask Him and then trust His guidance. He will assist you. Patience is the key. You probably will not know at first, but something will tell you whether or not to continue a relationship with that person. Listen for that small voice speaking to you. He wants you to heed to this advice.

When I want to get my students' attention, I say, "Stop, look, listen, and think." They use hand gestures while they repeat these words. When I have their attention, I speak.

Look for negative or positive feelings while you are around them. If at any point in the relationship you begin to feel uncomfortable, that is a sign. That's the time to move on before things become too entangled. Trust Him to send you the right person. This is the perfect time to focus on your children and begin to build your peaceful home. You all will be glad you did.

God has some angel people to assist you along the way. Look back at Goethe's couplet—a whole stream of events issues from that decision.

So many people have assisted me along the way. There have been unforeseen incidents, meetings, and material assistance that have occurred only by the hand of God. So will it be for you—if you let Him.

This is the ideal place to introduce a friend, and mentor, Dr. Sheary Johnson who introduced me to Pam Willis. Pam is our personal fitness instructor. This association caused me to become fit through exercise, nutrition, and spiritual guidance. She can assist you as you seek knowledge about how to become physically and spiritually fit. We are to be like Jesus in every way. He doesn't want us to be unhealthy, because that brings on all sorts of illness and disease.

The picture of health, she is a model of excellent health and has not one ounce of fat on her body. I can't say that about myself—yet.

Pam is a certified personal trainer with fifteen years experience. She is AFFA and ISCA certified in Pilates, yoga, high-low impact, step, and body and pump. She has a bachelor's degree in health and wellness with a minor in nutrition from Kaplan University. Pam was also an IPA Pro Figure Competitor for ten years. She attained pro status in August, 2010. She is also an at-home personal trainer and nutritional counselor (pamstotalfitness@gmail.com).

I included Pam's fitness and health in this section to add to our First Lady's initiative on the importance of becoming healthy. It must begin at home. Make it work for you. Have your own competition and go for family runs around the block.

Remember to be healthy; you must do what is necessary to have good health. If we are careful to make sound decisions, do the things necessary to support these decisions, we will have peaceful, healthy homes.

I couldn't leave this section without the words to back up and solidify the importance of looking and trusting in the Lord. Trust in the Lord with all your heart. Lean not unto your own understanding. In all your ways, acknowledge Him, and He will make your path straight. Be a doer of the Word and you can have your heart's desire (Prov. 3:5, NIV).

It is my desire to bridge the gap between home and school. Much love, time, money, and effort has been spent over the years for this cause. My research shows many people investing in our children.

Parents, please don't unwittingly cause your own children to fail. How you act speaks volumes to your children. They watch your every move and emulate your speech, actions, and reactions.

I was wondering why our parents were never called to school because of our behavior. I remember coming home from elementary school and telling my mom something the teacher had done to me.

She acted as though she had not heard me. She said, "Pat, what did you do?"

I said, "Nothing."

"Pat, what did you do?"

"Nothing."

After about five times, I realized she wasn't going any further than that.

Finally, I told her what I had done. Parents know their children and what they are capable of doing.

I had done the same thing at home. There was no need to take my side or contact the school. She knew I wouldn't do it again.

Boundaries were set at home that we knew we should not cross. We knew the long arm of the law reached right into the classroom. There was a healthy respect of the rules set at home. We did get spankings or whippings, but we were not abused.

The whippings were not done maliciously. We were never beaten or slapped. We broke rules and suffered the consequences at home, in the community, at church, or wherever we might be.

Do you remember acting up and suddenly feeling that someone was watching you? "Mama eyes" caused us to stop in our tracks and think about what the consequences were going to be when we got home.

We knew our parents had begun to bridge the gap between what was expected of us. There was no guessing. Bad manners and disrespect were not tolerated anywhere. Over the years, I have heard teachers say, "I'm going to call your mother." The child hollers, "I don't care! Tell her—she ain't gonna do nothing!"

Parents, you do your child a disservice when you just take their word without checking into it! Parents rarely say, "Yep. It's just like Sean. He does these same things at home. I will take care of it at home."

You know they will. The proof is that little Sean doesn't continue causing disruptions during the teaching time or any other time at school.

One morning, I saw a mother dragging her little boy down the hall. She was walking so fast that his little legs couldn't keep up. She did not slow down to help him keep up. He was screaming! She was screaming loudly and using profanity! I couldn't help but think she forgot she was at school! When she saw me coming down the hall, she did not lower her voice or stop the profanity.

"Calling me from my job about this '*expletive*'."

I felt so sad for the little boy; he was a preschooler or in kindergarten. I wondered what she might do to him when she got him in the car and then at home. My heart wrenched for him. This is what he lived with on a daily basis! He was acting just like his mama. Neither of them knew how to control themselves. Whatever he had done must have been pretty bad! It was still early morning, and the teacher needed to have him go back home! That woman did not realize what she had done to her son. How sad. He was emulating her actions.

Moms, dads, caregivers, Stop, look, and listen! What are you doing to your children? You can and must change!

If you empower your children at home, they will have no need to control or bully others at home, school, or anywhere else. They will know who they are and therefore value themselves and others. You cannot belittle your children and expect them to feel valued. You make them feel little inside.

When children don't feel valued, they hurt inside—and they will hurt those around them. Hurt children hurt other children. Hurt people hurt other people. That's what they have been taught—and that's what they do.

Incarcerated girls and boys wish someone had cared! Caring, loving, and kindness should not be that hard—especially for our own offspring.

Whatever you expect to happen at school must begin at home. What you allow at home will be exhibited at school negatively or positively. Teach manners, discipline, and character at home for positive experiences at school.

You will see these words often: **be, do, have**. They must be in order. Teach sharing. How? You show them sharing. Use the word you want them to know. You are **be**-ing a **do**-er of the word.

"Tim, come here. Let Mom share this pizza with you. Show me how you can share your cookies with me, your brother and sister." You are be-ing a do-er. Now they have what you shared. All have benefited. You are learning to teach by example. You taught loving and kindness at the same time. They will follow your example at home, school, and other places.

Teach them respect by letting them see you being respectful to their siblings. Use the word respect often as you are talking with them. Say, "John, it's awesome to see how you respect so-and-so. That deserves a big pat on the back and an extra treat: Your choice."

I hope you are getting the picture. You must do this with whatever you are teaching. Use the words: responsibility, trust, honesty, compassion, and forgiveness and other values.

As you continue these actions, you will automatically think up ways to build a positive relationship with each other. It will go with them wherever they happen to be. We have no more time to waste. Start at home. The meetings will help you set up strategies on how you will operate your home. If the effort is not started at home, you will continue to see the problems, issues, and devastation of our children and youth accelerate even more.

Look at your house and decide what you want your home to look like in the future. Please don't close your eyes. Look, see, act. Commit yourself and your family. Start the process and the benefits will last. The pieces of the puzzle will come together. You will be glad you did. Your family will be glad you did because peace will reign at your address. The butterflies on each page are reminders of the beautiful, peaceful home you are building for your family.

Unless there is a mental or physical deficiency, all children can learn. Even the ones mentioned above can learn something. Children will not earn good grades or be successful in school or elsewhere without commitment. They must study and follow directions at school and at home. Becoming disciplined is the key. You must set an example for them to follow.

If they do these things, they will be the best they can be. Parents must do everything in their power to raise healthy, well-rounded children. It is your responsibility.

Since you are now their hero or "shero," you can get them to do anything, but you must remember to go first. They must see you being about the business of starting healthy eating habits.

Once you get started, they will also become healthy eaters. You will start by changing how you shop and how you prepare your food. There are reasons for the need to change. The reasons are for the health of your children. We have been hearing about how our food intake can cause us to be healthy or unhealthy.

No parent wants a child to develop disease and illness from an improper diet, yet that's the dilemma. We don't want to have this happen to our children, yet statistics prove that to be true. There is hope and much help out there. We must become disciplined and committed to addressing the tremendous effect that nutrition can play in our children's educational process.

First Lady Michelle Obama has been championing and leading the charge to stamp out childhood obesity in the United States. She said, "Parents and caregivers play a key role in not only making healthy choices for themselves, but in today's world, this isn't easy. *Let's Move!* offers parents and caregivers the tools, support, and information they need to make healthier choices while instilling eating habits in children that will last a lifetime."

Michelle Obama's healthy food campaign states that one-third of young people are overweight or obese. One-third suffers from diabetes at some point in their lives. In the Latino and black communities, those numbers go up to 150 percent.

According to a study from the Kaiser Foundation, children spend seven hours a day using some kind of media device, school lunches are fattier, school gym classes are shorter and or nonexistent, and the erosion of 1950s neighborhood culture means the days of playing outside are gone. Thanks to Michelle Obama, many schools are changing to healthier lunches and are including more exercise in their daily schedules.

As I teach at different schools in Richmond, it is wonderful to see more fresh fruit and vegetables—and less fats and sugars—served at lunch. Richmond is not the only school district that has taken the challenge to serve more nutritious lunches.

Since God made all living creatures, we are all important. We should take care of our species. We come together to save our cheetahs, whales, dolphins, and eagles. **Our childrenare no less important!**

Thank you again, First Lady Michelle Obama, for leading the pack to save our children through the support of the Child Nutrition Bill. Thank you to the House and the Senate for a bipartisan vote. This effort proves we can come together on important issues for the children—and for the people.

Taking School Home

When God gives you a vision or a plan for your life, you can't run away from the vision. It will follow you, lead you, and direct you to get to it—even if it takes years. "I know the plans I have for you, . . . , plans to prosper you and not to harm you, plans to give you hope and a future" (Jer. 29:11, NIV).

Once we "get over ourselves" and trust His words and do what He puts in our hearts, nothing can stop us! Even when we doubt God and His word, He knows that one day we will "get it." We will "do it." We will stop fighting and follow His plans for our lives. That's where I was stuck for years. I finally became a doer and not a hearer only of His words.

"Before you were formed, in your mother's womb, I saw you and approved you" (Jer. 1:5, NIV). If God saw me before I was born and approved me—and approved of what I would finally become—I must get to it. I will follow the plan He has for my life."

He took what has always been in my heart all of my life—a deep love of children and a compassion for teaching them—even after I tried to retire a number of times. He had a plan for me, for my future, and for the children's future. I could feel in my spirit that I hadn't finished my work.

God impressed upon me to take school into the home where I could assist more students each year. I signed up as a permanent substitute with the Richmond Public Schools and began teaching in many schools.

I was told by parents at conference, meetings, on the phone, and in the PTA that they were pleased with how my efforts helped their children. Many parents said, "I wish I could take you home even for a weekend." Soon I started to conduct workshops on a peaceful home.

The Spirit kept urging me to go wider, reach higher, and look deeper. This went on for years, but I wasn't listening. "Enlarge the place of your tent, stretch your tent curtains wide, do not hold back; lengthen your cords, strengthen your stakes. For you will spread out to the right and to the left; . . ." (Isa. 54:2-3a, NIV).

It became clear that this book was my next step. I had to take school into homes to help parents and children see what goes on in schools—and how they can utilize those skills at home.

You can send your children to school properly equipped to learn. "Commit to the Lord whatever you do and your plans will succeed" (Prov. 16:13, NIV).

Family meetings are necessary to learn what's going on in the home and realizing how powerful the family is as a unit. "Two are better than one, because they have a good return for their work; if one falls down, his friend can help him up" (Eccl. 4:9-10, 12, NIV).

Though one may be overpowered, two can defend themselves. A cord of three strands is not easily broken. The family unit working as a team is an example of this verse.

We are God's beloved and we should clothe ourselves with compassion, kindness, humility, gentleness, and patience. We should forgive each other as God has forgiven us. Above all, these virtues put on love which binds us all in perfect unit (Col. 3:12-14, NIV). Who would dare to argue with that?

God teaches us how to love because love changes things. I believe we can all attest to the fact that much of the world's ills have occurred because of the lack of love. True love cannot hurt.

I say, "Hurt people hurt people." I teach this repeatedly to my students. After a few times of not accepting this negative behavior, they finally get it. I do not allow it! After I get up on my soapbox a few times, they get the point and will not allow it in their classroom. They like their peaceful classroom and will work together to preserve it.

Taking a look into the classroom will also give you strategies at home to combat disruptions that break the peace at home. Let me tell you what happens at the beginning of each school when I enter as a substitute. When the students enter the room, I look to see if they come in and follow the teacher's routine or if they take advantage of the situation. I watch for the ones who come in sit down and begin working. I go over to them and whisper a compliment about their ability to be responsible. I write their names on the board and put a point behind their names.

Listening for words of respect, thank you, sorry, etc., I compliment their manners. I call these RAK (Random Acts of Kindness) points. By this time, they are curious. They put two and two together, put their heads down, and begin to work. They want to get RAK points. They like to see their names in lights. This works for all but about two in the class. By the end of the day, most of their names are on the board. I tell them I will leave their names on the board for the teacher and she or he will reward their behavior. These strategies bring a sense of pride and peace that we will have a great day.

A few don't—or can't—get their names on the board, or they have to get their names erased for not following directions. I give them three or four chances to make up the points, looking for the smallest thing to give them a chance. If I see them almost do the right thing, I might say, "I know you were about to pick up that piece of paper that just fell beside your desk." Even if they know I saw them throw the paper on the floor, I have built a special rapport with that student. They have seen me do a RAK. I have seen them accidentally drop pencils and other objects on the floor and they say, "Ms. Braxton, Mike dropped this pencil, and I want to give it to him."

Mike will thank him, knowing it was no accident. However, they both got RAK points. They are just practicing. Just before dismissal, I have another meeting to discuss the successful day. I let them know that I saw the paper and pencil incidents and know they were practicing being good.

I say, *"Act the way you want to be and soon you'll be the way you act."* We must model at home what we want to see at home, and they will act accordingly at school and other places.

Children want to follow directions. They won't tell you that, but they will respond in such a way that you know they appreciate it. They will give you a hug, write you a note, or show they appreciate you.

In all classes, I take about ten minutes in the morning to explain the point system and discuss the behavior I expect. I discuss respect, responsibility, compassion, and other values. This meeting of minds and expectations builds lasting relationships.

Over the years, many incidents are repeated—and I almost always know the outcome. As I was discussing the point system and rewards at the end of the day, someone hurt someone else's feelings. I informed them that no one in Ms. Braxton's classes was allowed to hurt another one's feelings. I talked about hurt people who hurt people and related it to animals who do not have the power to think as humans. Why do animals seem to know what humans don't know? I mentioned the Virginia Tech massacre and what was behind the killings. Cho had many pains in his life that had not been addressed. He hurt—so he hurt people. I was trying to touch their hearts to stir up some love.

At recess, a few angry students were fussing about a kickball game. They didn't get to finish the game because I brought them inside to have a meeting about what happened. After the discussion, one student went over to the people he had been fussing with and apologized to each of them. This caused others to do likewise. They shook hands; high-fived each other, smiled, and hugged. I had a few tears in my eyes. When it was time for the buses to be called, they left with their heads held high because they knew they had shown compassion for each other.

The next day, I saw their teacher. They had already told her about their day and how wonderful they felt about their points for following directions, listening, and completing all assigned work left by the teacher.

I have used this technique in every class—from kindergarten to grade five. I am amazed that all students embrace it and want to know when I am coming back. I have learned how important building a positive relationship is because children don't care how much you know until they know how much you care. They must know that home is a place where they are loved and cared for and that they matter. The point system will be discussed in depth later in the chapter on the family meeting

I love to recite the poem "I Am Somebody" (see Appendix V) and have students recite it behind me. I like to watch their faces as they recite it with emphasis on "I am somebody." They smile as I tell them I see doctors, lawyers, preachers, nurses, teachers, principals, entrepreneurs, professional athletes, actors, actresses, policemen and policewomen, and firefighters. I give them two sticky notes and ask them to write what they want to be. One will stay on their desk to remind them of their future goals. The other one is to be given to the teacher to remind them of the promise they made to themselves.

When I see them begin to act up, I say, "Now, do you think Dr. (their name) would act like that?" This makes them think about what they wrote. They are starting to process it in their minds.

I say, "*Act the way you want to be and soon you'll be the way you act.*"

They start to raise their heads a little higher. They walk down the hall, standing a little taller. I have had some onlookers comment about their new look. Pride is shown on all their faces. Because this was the first time all six of the kindergarteners walked down the hall in one straight quiet line, I asked the principal to announce it over the intercom. When he did, the class just beamed.

I hope you will see the importance of your words when you speak to children, about children, and before children. Reckless words pierce like a sword, but the tongue of the wise brings healing (Prov. 12:18, NIV). If this can be accomplished with entire classes, it certainly can be done with a few children at home. This chapter will help you accomplish this. As you take a glance at these strategies, you will see their simplicity and use them to build a peaceful home.

You will see the absolute validity of the importance of the home-school relationship for building our children and youth from within. When the positive change is internal, it cannot be easily erased.

You will soon notice that when the parent, teacher, and student are in close contact—by phone, Internet, or conference—a rapport has been established. Happy parents, happy children, and happy teachers result in a win-win situation for all concerned. It endows the student with the ability to soar in school.

This school-home relationship is an equilateral triangle where there are no broken lines of communication between the parent, teacher, and student. (See Appendix VIII)

Intervention and Prevention

After reading a few chapters in this guide, you know my intentions are to prevent the issues, problems, and destruction from continuing at home and school.

Things are so bad in my house! I can't keep them from happening? I have tried everything!

You have not tried everything. There are always new avenues on which to travel. The answers are out there.

How bad do you want it? Are you really ready to try something different?

As you already know, it has been difficult, to say the least. You may be at the point where you think it's impossible. Jesus looked at them and said, "With man this is impossible but not with God all things are possible with God" (Mk. 10:27, NIV).

The meetings address negative issues. The goal is to inhibit continued destruction in the family. *A Parent's Guide to a Peaceful Home* was written to intercede and mediate. You will realize that the level of difficulty drops off as you make the effort to change.

Once you make the changes, I hope you won't go back to the way it used to be. Once peace enters your home, your family will want to keep it that way.

My research carried me to so much heart-wrenching information about what has happened to millions of young men and young women whose potential was robbed from them through incarceration, gangs, and death. I think about the millions and millions of families who have been affected over the years. It is astounding! It is staggering! The sad part is we let it happen—and we keep letting it happen! Some young children have multiple families incarcerated. When will it end?

We are in the end times when Jesus comes back for his Church. Let us be ". . . so doing . . ." (Matt.24:46, NIV) what He instructed us to do. We can do our part to fix what we can fix together, starting with our children.

At Reid Elementary, each teacher taught character values to their students, and they were incorporated in every aspect of the school. After five years, the kindergarten students had been taught and trained in the five core values (respect, responsibility, caring, trust, and family) on a daily basis. These positive habits had been established at school and home. As they moved through the grades, each teacher continued to reinforce the core values.

The families were involved. The positive habits and behavior caused them to become well-rounded students. Their grades continued to improve. Many of them are having a positive effect on society—not to mention the jobs and professions they now have. All of us at Reid came together for the sake of our children.

We teachers and staff at G.H. Reid Elementary celebrated Black History month in many ways. The students celebrated by "becoming" various notable Black men and women which culminated in a Festival,Feast and a PTA Meeting. The teachers and staff also participated by dressing in African attire for the whole month. This picture was one of those occasions as the students had just entered the building for the beginning of the school day, this was also the time that the Community of Caring was in operation at our school.

I must relate what I have seen in some schools in our city. I also know that what I am about to say is happening in many schools in the United States. The media reports on bullying and murder. Could any school or family in the world want that? I don't think so.

Many students who exhibited unacceptable behavior in kindergarten continued to exhibit negative behaviors in the upper grades. Now they are more cunning, divisive, angry, disrespectful, irresponsible, uncaring, and hurtful. These students refuse to follow directions and want to be in charge.

It is difficult for the teacher to teach for the prescribed time for each subject; therefore, all students suffer. Much of the irresponsible behavior occurs because they have not learned—and they distract the whole class.

They know what they are doing, but they can't explain it. I have had this conversation with them. They always say they don't know. I believe them.

I have them to fill out the "Think Sheet" (see Appendix). It's hard for them to admit what they did without accusing someone else first. I have them rewrite it until they can tell me what they did. This is very cleansing. It is not for me to fuss at them. It is an opening for honest discussion.

The Think Sheet is for intervention and prevention. As an intervention tool, it permits me to be a mediator to intervene in such a way as to bring closure to the situation. As a preventive tool, it helps me nip the situation in the bud. They hate the Think Sheet! Of course, there are consequences. Don't worry—there is no bloodletting. Not being allowed to participate in recess is close to bloodletting in their minds. Missing the stickers or treats at the end of the day causes them to apologize.

It's important to let the punishment fit the crime. You must find out what will hurt them the most, cause them to think, and prevent recurring offenses. A child should not continue the same negative behavior from birth through adulthood.

A child who continues to fail over a period of years apparently does not have the necessary family support to build a strong inner self-worth. These are the children we see struggling in our classrooms throughout the USA. They are looking for someone to assist, validate and pick them up. The adults should be the "picker-uppers."

Many students are interacting negatively. They disrupt the class because they need to be a part of something! They realized at an early age that these actions bring attention to them. Being so young, they are not aware that they may be building lifelong negative character traits. It takes an experienced eye to recognize that they are not bad; they need to be redirected and disciplined in a positive manner. You are capable of doing this. You have help in this guide. The strategies in this guide may not work for every child, but they will for most. These negative behaviors have been recognized at home. There may have been interventions that did not work.

During conferences, many parents explain that they are at a loss about how to get their children to listen and follow directions. *I just don't know what to do. I have tried everything! Nothing I do has worked! They are in trouble all the time at home and school. What can I do?*

Carlita Alford-Jones, a mother, teacher and friend, resolved reoccurring problems with a daughter who had many issues at home and at school. She had tried everything. Nothing seemed to faze her daughter. She was very frustrated.

Mrs. Jones promised a spa day with her daughters to get manicures and pedicures. The daughter with the "I-don't-care" attitude acted as if she wanted her mom to beg her.

Through her frustration, she took her daughter home, fixed her a sandwich, gave her a drink, and left her with her friend while the rest of them went to a nice restaurant. They stayed out a long time. When they came back, they were overjoyed, smiling, and talking about the wonderful time. This hurt her enough to rethink her attitude. She is now thinking before the attitude shows up.

As I listened to her, she had no idea that I was writing a book that had the same preventive solution in my guide. I call it "The Emergency Pack." It is a form of tough love that works.

What you have just read are issues, situations, and habits that people have learned over a period of time. They are hard to break—but not impossible.

I have three short stories about animal behavior and human behavior. These are true stories about how human beings have trained animals and how people do things out of habit.

A gentleman visited Africa to see a group of mammoth elephants. They were lined up and chained by one leg to a peg in the ground. The man marveled at all the elephants not daring to move too far from the stakes.

The man asked the trainer why the elephants just stood there when it was obvious that they could effortlessly break the small chain and pull up the stake.

The trainer said that, as babies, the elephants were chained or roped by a stake in the ground. They tried over and over to break away, but the force had caused their legs to become raw and painful.

After a while, they did not try to break away anymore. Lesson learned. The adult elephants remember the pain and—even though they could break away—the fear of pain keeps them in bondage.

Another man went on the road with the circus. His act was jumping fleas that no longer jumped. Fleas like to jump high onto whatever surface on which they see a bite to eat. His fleas would not jump out of the container even though the container had no top.

Everyone who visited the show asked, "Why don't they even try to jump out?"

The fleas had generational training that followed the family of fleas for a long while. The first trainees had put the fleas in a container with a top on it. Each time the fleas tried to jump up and out, they hit the top. *Ouch, that hurts!* After trying a thousand times, they stopped trying to jump out.

The trainer had trained them. *It hurts when we try to jump up there, so we will just stay down here on the bottom of the container.* Even after a period of time, the generation of fleas did not try to jump out—even though there was no top.

One Christmas, a wife was preparing a ham for dinner. Her husband asked, "Why do you always cut the top off of the ham before you put it in the oven?" The wife said, "I don't know. I always see Mother do it."

When they went to her Mother's house with the ham, the son-in-law asked her about it.

She said, "I don't know why she does it. I cut the top off because it's too large to go in the oven!"

We are creatures of habit like the animals. The habit does not even have to make sense to humans. We do it because we learned it from others.

My reason for telling these stories is to cause us to think about what we have taught our children—even inadvertently. Sometimes we don't know what we have taught our children through our negative or positive behaviors. We prefer to think we taught them positive behaviors only. Not so. They are a reflection of us.

During conferences, some parents say, "I don't know where they got that bad habit. I didn't teach my child to do or say such things."

One mother became unglued when I called and explained that her fourth grader had done no work, kept getting out of his seat without permission, and was touching students. Her son had been used to running the class.

She raised her voice and said, "I expletive, expletive didn't raise my children like that! I will beat his expletive when he gets home! Oh, I'm so sorry. I didn't mean to say those words."

She kept apologizing. I made no comment. I asked her to come for a visit without telling him.

She must have done something. When I went to substitute in that class, he said, "Ms. Braxton, I'm going to be good today." He stayed in his seat and did his work.

I have no idea if he was just well-behaved for me or if he always behaved this way for his classroom teacher. I must ask her the next time I see her.

Before I leave this chapter, I will leave some staggering statistics. I hope these breathtaking statistics will cause people who are in charge of God's children to stop, look, listen, think, and take action.

Take positive action in your homes, schools, churches, organizations, and community. In "You Are a Marvel," (see Appendix III) Pablo Casals says, "You are unique, a marvel. Then can you harm another, who is like you, a marvel?

Remember, if we expect things to change, we must be the change agents. President Obama said, "We are the change we seek."

Let us intervene with an eye to prevent the continuous hurting of children. I have included some incidents that document abuse, neglect, failure of educational programs, social issues, drug use and abuse, violence, emotional issues, and racial profiling. The following list is taken directly from the Internet.

- CNN May 17, 2011 Please Don't Fail Me Now
- Press Review News Wire—Communities in Schools
- Documentary: Waiting for Superman—Best Documentary, National Board of Review
- Up until 1970, United States schools were the best in the world. We led the world 40-50 years ago. Now we are behind most nations, even third world countries.
- Now we are at 25 percent in math; 17 percent to 21 percent in science, 14 percent in reading scores are from fifteen year olds.
- Schools have become drop out factories—6,000-7,000 a day, says Steve Barr and Bill Strickland. Secretary of Education Arne Duncan says that is 10,000,000 a year!
- 68 percent of the inmates are dropouts. New prisons are being built according to fourth-grade black boys' test scores. Three more prisons are being built than public schools. Ninety million plus people are incarcerated. See References. Dr. Kunjusa, *Raising Black Boys*
- Incarceration and reincarnation recidivism continues to occur. One young man had been back in prison seventeen times, and he was still a young adult.
- There are about 820,000 teenage pregnancies each year. The main rise is in teenagers younger than fifteen—they have at least two to three more children before the age of twenty.
- Teenagers have killed their parents.
- One teen shot his principal and assistant principal then killed himself. Other teachers and principals have been murdered in high schools and universities.
- Father burns up sons and himself.
- Father burns up daughters and himself.
- A student went into cafeteria and shot students that he did not know.
- Eleven-year-old girl kills ten-year-old girl.
- Young mother put infant in microwave oven and turned it on.
- Young mothers drowned their children by either driving or pushing car in lake.
- Students bullied students to the point that they committed suicide.

- Large numbers of students are murdered at our high schools and universities over the years.
- There are a large number of our babies, children, young adults, adults, and whole families murdered because of the rise and sale of drugs.

This may seem like overkill, but I want to cause deep compassion and the taking of positive action toward changing these conditions. Creating peaceful homes is one way parents can initiate change, beginning at the beginning.

Hurt people hurt people. There are millions and even billions of people hurting because of the tragic loss of babies, children, youth, adults, families, aunts, uncles, cousins, and friends. I think I included everybody.

Each year, I ask my students if they have been hurt by the incarceration of family members. I do this so that I might know what concerns them the most. This helps me know and show compassion for their feelings and why they may be acting out.

In the seventies, there were one or two hands raised.

In the eighties and nineties, there were never more than five hands raised.

From 2000-2012, every child—including the teacher—raised our hands. All of us are affected. No one is exempt.

During our class meetings, the children were very open about their feelings concerning incarcerated parents. When they give deep information, I stop them. I tell them they don't need to give details. Sometimes they really want to talk in detail. I tell them that I will get the counselor to help them with their feelings. Sometimes they tell me anyway.

I do not let them go into deep detail so classmates do not make fun of them. They wrestle with it and can't understand why it happened. This is a sad, sad plight for them.

Many visit parents at the prisons. When they come to school on Monday, I know that they had a difficult weekend. I see it in their demeanor.

If people having problems with their children would make a paradigm shift, a change of mind, and a heart—to make their homes a safe haven for all children—it would bring about the peaceful home everyone would cherish.

After reading the statistics above, what I'm asking cannot be too much! We can at least make the place where we dwell with our families a place where all can thrive.

> These commandments that I give you today are to be upon your hearts. Impress them on your children. Talk to them when you get up, when you sit at home, and when you walk or drive along the road.
>
> Tie them as symbols on your hands and bind them on your foreheads. Write them on the door frames of your house and on your gates. (Deut. 6:6-9, NIV)

These scriptures are telling us the importance of training and remembering to live them out beginning at home and every place we go.

Never forget they're always watching! I guess I can say they're our unofficial watchdogs. Watch out!

If I sound like a nanny, I make myself the Grand Nanny of all who will desire to make life better for your family. That is why I speak to you as your nanny would. We are in this together.

We are intervening through the family meetings to prevent our children from disaster in the future. Our children are what we say and what we speak over them. Let's speak God's blessings over each of our children—blessings of health, peace, fulfillment of potential, success, and prosperity. They are God's children. Make it your business to read this or your own blessings over them in the family meeting setting.

Teach them to call themselves smart, intelligent, and kind. Use those character words. At first, they will repeat them because you said them; however, the words will become a part of them—just as the negative words stuck to them before.

Have them call each other these words and the positive words you gave them.

Act the way you want to be—and soon you'll be the way you act.

No Child Left Behind and Annual Yearly Progress (AYP)

The failure of our children in education and society can be laid at all of our feet. However, as you have read in this guide and heard from the media, there are numerous brothers and sisters who saw the need, felt the need to assist our children, and decided that they are our brother's keepers.

I address this section to the parents, caregivers, communities, churches, schools, city, state, the Department Of Education, and the federal government who have a vested interest in educating our kids.

Many of the issues have trickled down from the federal government. I speak about President Bush's No Child Left Behind Act 1958 and Annual Yearly Progress (AYP).

These words sound noble. The real truth is that many four- and five-year-olds come into schools already behind. It has been almost impossible to catch them up in one year.

There are many variables that prevent AYP. Many four- and five-year-olds have not come to school prepared. They are already handicapped. They are not equipped and have almost no social skills. Many did not attend preschool. They have no clue about school.

To make matters worse many, kindergarten classes are overcrowded with up to twenty-five students per teacher. Many of them have no assistance. Sometimes there are part-time aides. I know this because I have taught in these classes. In my experience, many elementary classes have more than twenty-five students and no assistants.

From the triangle base to the apex represents students who came to school already trained and disciplined. This was about twenty-three students. No more than three students caused distractions. These students may have had some mental handicap or social malfunction.

The teacher could do what they were trained to do—teach. We had no murders in our schools.

This triangle has flipped upside down with the base at the top representing the twenty-five students. Sad to say that only two to five of them are trained and disciplined at home. If you think this is an exaggeration, look at our test scores. Look at our ranking in education compared to other nations whose students are outranking ours in science, math, and reading.

You can also volunteer to assist. What would you see? The majority of these disruptive students in the classrooms, cafeterias, and halls have no regard for any adult or their behavior. Bullying, fighting, profanity, and murders are rampant.

Look at what Mr. V. Lang reported on Education Nation on September 28, 2010. "If teachers could get back to teaching instead of trying to discipline and stop bad behavior, we would have much more success."

Teachers have been called "glorified babysitters." If this is the way you feel, please help! I believe that would be the only way for you to see for yourself. You would feel compelled to help.

Let us do our part to assist in helping to change the system and the way we educate our children.

Teachers have gotten a bad rap and reputation. I hope you will become an advocate and help in some way. These are our children in our villages.

Some teachers are burnt out and should find other options. There are some who are in the wrong profession just as other people sometimes choose the wrong professions.

The shameful part of this is the powers that be have never thought it important enough to pay teachers what they are worth. Do you not know that everyone who received an education and is making any money up to the millions and trillions of dollars came through some teaching?

I have taught thousands of students who have jobs and professions—multiply that by all the teachers who have ever taught. The student numbers and the salaries are astronomical.

Will you who read this deny this is true? Many teachers are fearful of losing their jobs so they will not speak out. I don't have to worry about that. I am a permanent substitute and my message box is filled to the maximum. I have to constantly turn down jobs.

I took many breaks to write this book for the parents, teachers, and administrators from the past and the future. Our collective voices must be heard so we can finally get some restitution.

One year, I decided to take a look at the amount of money I had already spent on school supplies for my students. It was over six hundred dollars—and school was not out yet! I know I am not the only teacher who has done that. The teacher store is overcrowded with us. We do this from the small salary we make for the love of our students.

My enjoyment comes from going to schools with treats, rewards, and certificates which come from the dollar store. Thank God for them! I call myself the "Dollar Store Queen!" I thought I needed to throw in a little humor because I was—and you may be—getting a little heated.

You will remember the variables mentioned that make it almost impossible to meet Annual Yearly Progress (AYP) and No Child Left Behind mandates. A lack of discipline at home and the class size at school with limited help was mentioned. This is coupled with the fact that approximately twenty of the twenty-five kindergarteners are not ready to learn. Their little educational slates have almost nothing on them. They have the giggles and ants in their pants and know almost nothing about giving, sharing, and kindness. On top of that, they whine and cry about everything!

To make matters worse, some of them will go off if they don't get their way! They throw temper tantrums, cuss, hit, bite, and throw whatever they can pick up at the teacher because she has class rules that all must follow. Some teachers have had to get tetanus shots. Sounds like a war zone—doesn't it?

On a few occasions, I have seen them fight the police when they were called. They had to be put in restraints to remove them from the school. They have no fear of authority. When you see actions such as this, you can't help but pray and hope they get help.

It is almost impossible to make AYP and ensure that no child is left behind. These children are not allowed to take naps anymore. Their recess may be fifteen to twenty minutes per day. The resource classes; music, art, physical education (PE), media, and Spanish are approximately forty minutes for each class per week. This is the time for the classroom teachers to prepare for the next day. Remember, I said this period of 40-45 minutes per day. What I remember is that this is never enough time. Many teachers do what I did for those forty years

I taught: Go to school early; stay late; take school work home; stay up until we fall asleep on the papers. The bad part is that we never feel that we have caught up. Does the teacher really have enough time to teach reading, math, science, and social studies to assure that no child is left behind? People blame the teachers because the children have not learned, but they have not been disciplined or trained at home. "Train up your child . . ." (Pr. 22:6, NIV). The Bible doesn't tell teachers to train up the children.

Trying to do both does not leave enough time to teach all subjects. Something is lacking. The teacher's job is to teach and instruct!

I don't want to forget about the one to five students whose parents have prepared them before they enter school. They have enrolled the children in daycare or preschool and have worked with them, disciplined them, and trained them at home.

Sadly, some parents think it's the teacher's job to do the teaching, disciplining, and training. One parent told me this when I called her to inform her of her child's behavior.

My hat goes off to extremely proficient teachers who labor tirelessly to meet the goals set for them by the federal and state government. In Richmond, they are called Standards of Learning Tests. There are quite a few objectives that must be mastered in order to move to the next grade level. That seems logical; however, there are teacher's tests, biweekly tests, nine-week tests, and the tests at the end of the year. There is almost no time left to review before it is time for the next test! Schools resemble factories. Push, push, push the products out there even though there may be inferior items.

Principals, teachers, and students are tired of mandates and constant testing to meet AYP and No Child Left Behind. Many students shut down.

Please don't forget all the variables that make it almost impossible to meet the requirements set by the state and federal government. Variables climb up from preschool, to kindergarten, primary school, middle school, and to high school. Many teachers are to be commended for their valiant effort to make it happen against all odds. The majority of their work is done in honesty—even though they look like they have worked in a coal mine as they leave their schools. That's a little West Virginia humor. I wanted to make you teachers smile.

Since this is my book, I can give my opinion. It is highly unfair to blame all teachers for low test scores given the circumstances. I am referring to the variables. Go back and read them if you forgot. Focusing on test scores and tying them to teacher salaries is highly unfair without changing the class size and offering help—especially in the kindergarten, first grade, and second grade.

How many of these children have had training and discipline at home? Possibly five of the students are so privileged. Do the math! It is easy to talk about, but difficult to teach twenty tots to read! It is unfair to the teachers and students. Who wants to be put in the ring with both hands tied behind them? Not many would be successful.

If teachers could select their own students, make sure they have good character and a high IQ along with parent participation, and are prepared for school, they can assuredly make AYP and meet No Child Left Behind standards.

My granddaughters were selected to go to Governor's schools for math, engineering, arts and science. They were selected because of their academic status and citizenship. They had maintained AYP and more. Their elementary years were spent in Faith Landmark Ministries' Victory Christian Academy. They were prepared at school and at home.

Without that base, most students will struggle, fail, cause disruptions, and fight. Many teachers do not have the experience and knowledge to know how to make it happen in spite of the odds.

Don't penalize the teachers without giving them the help they need! Teachers and students need a character education program to help change bad character to good character, especially when it has not been done at home.

I taught preschool and kindergarten for two years. There was no way I could have gotten through it without the help of two highly experienced and proficient teachers, Gloria Brown. and Alice Lilly. I want to commend them and all teachers for their efforts.

While teaching kindergarten, I didn't have a clue about what to do. I was not used to giving instructions eighteen times and having them look at you like does in the headlights. I was confused. I think about how new teachers feel when they tackle preschool, kindergarten, and the lower grades.

Here is a secondhand look at two classes of prekindergarten and kindergarten. I will give you the short version. The full version of what happened could become its own book—*Look Out Here They Come! HELP!*

I was alone with eighteen kindergarteners in September; all of them had to go to the restroom at the same time. One of them started to wiggle; soon, all were wiggling. I knew all of them didn't have to go, but what could I do? They lied or told fibs or tales. You pick one.

There was one restroom in the class, so I had to take them all down the hall. The boys' and girls' restrooms were far from each other. I told them to line up. They didn't know what that meant. Putting the girls in one line and the boys in the other, I turned my back to check if my two lines were in order. After one second, they had scattered like ants! Panic arose because I didn't know one name. It was early September.

Praying was in order! I started to pray! I have lost some children! God answered my prayer! I finally gathered all of them. They did use the restroom. I made it through that day. Happiness is not having to call eighteen parents to come to school with dry clothes. I made it through!

It would have helped if I had had some assistance. One of us could have taken a group of boys or girls. While taking them back to the classroom, I envisioned the headlines in bold print: "Richmond Elementary Teacher Loses 18 Kids!"

Two years prior, a similar situation occurred with Mrs. Gloria Brown's fifteen preschoolers. We were going to recess. They were lined up ready to go out, and someone called my name. Looking away to see who it was, and immediately turning back, they had scattered again! I found one, put him in line, and said, "Stand right here!"

Each time I would get one, the others scattered again. I said, "Where did they go?" I finally gathered them up and proceeded to go outside. I wondered how I would get them back inside!

I have taught many little kids since that first experience and have learned a great deal thanks to Gloria and Alice, my pre-school and kindergarten mentors.

New and inexperienced teachers and parents, don't be afraid to ask for help. That's how we learn. Look for the individuals who have experience in what you need. They will be glad you asked. You will have less stress.

In kindergarten, repetition, recitation and routine are the keys. Eighteen or twenty students put away their backpacks, homework/ behavior folder in the container, and sit at tables or on the rug to wait for instructions.

The teacher leads the students as they sing opening songs. They sit on the carpet in their assigned spaces. We say "Crisscross, Applesauce, hands in your lap." This is crucial. Discipline is being taught here. If the children learn these routine lessons, much progress can be made. However, many teachers have to constantly repeat the same things. "Keep your hands in your lap. Keep your hands off your classmate. Keep your feet to yourself."

You hear crying. A child says, "Teacher, she stepped on my hands."

We say, "That's the reason we tell you to keep your hands in your lap!"

A student says, "Teacher, he kicked me."

We say, "That's why we tell you to sit crisscross."

You are trying to get through the gathering, which includes reading, science, social studies, and math. I was amazed when I saw how this was done. The days of the week, the months, the seasons, the weather, and the choice of clothing for the day were an introduction to science and social studies.

Math included counting the days in school by using a calendar. They learned multiplication and counting by ones, twos, fives and tens. They learn patterns using colors and shapes and counting money. They learned about presidents, President's Day, and which president's face is on which bills or coins. The alphabet chart helped them begin to read—first by singing the ABCs and learning the sounds.

There was so much more. The beginning lasted about thirty minutes. Ten to fifteen minutes were taken to correct behavior. While the students remained on the carpet, the teacher prepared to begin the language block. It lasted about two hours. They went to the restroom and got water during a ten-minute break.

The students were now getting antsy and wiggly. We had to keep stopping to correct behavior. For that reason, some teachers take "wiggle breaks."

I will now transition into one of my first experiences as a kindergarten teacher.

While my kindergartners were sitting on the carpet, I began to introduce the lesson. I read a connecting story with follow-up questions using who? What? When? Where? Why? and How? This was comprehension. There was much more.

When it was time to prepare them for their assigned work at three or four stations, they were to complete assignments based on the day's lesson. I guided them through each assignment by asking them to repeat what they were to do. It took me almost until June to get it to run smoothly.

Some experienced teachers have it and they're on it! I, a veteran teacher, never got there that smoothly. It was surprising how much they had learned. I kept forgetting they were not fourth and fifth graders.

Preschool and kindergarten is not the best place to introduce a new or inexperienced teacher to new students. Those tots need an efficient, experienced teacher and an assistant.

The students were ready to go to their stations for fifteen or twenty minutes. A bell rang, and they were told to clean up their areas, line up, and take their belongings to the next station. This was repeated three or four times, depending on the number of students. The ideal group was four or five students. They were to do it quietly because I was at the teacher's table with four or five students. The students I was teaching were constantly looking at whose group was fussing while moving to the next station.

I was interrupted any number of times while all kinds of distractions and disturbances occurred. This blocked learning. I had to stop with my group to attend to the distractions.

Ms. Braxton, he took my crayon, pencil, paper, book, glue. She keeps kicking me under the table. Oh, Ms. Braxton, he said a bad word! She keeps looking at me! He fell out of his chair and hit his head. He has a knot or blood running.

Someone had to watch my class while I took the child to the nurse. Parents asked, "Where was the teacher?" I was in the room with a small group—far away from the accident.

Most of the time, I didn't see what happened because their group was supposed to be working—not playing, pushing, and taking things! We ask parents to discipline, and train them to follow instructions at home. Teachers cannot be everywhere at the same time! We're not God!

I am surprised that more students are not hurt. Angels are watching over them!

One incident worth recalling was when they were to cut and paste certain objects in specific places to match things. They were using glue—not glue sticks. I instructed them to use two to three dots of glue on each object.

"Ms. Braxton, there's glue on the table."

I left my group to see what happened? He was coming toward me with glue running down his face, shirt, pants, and tennis shoes. I didn't know what to clean up first and I didn't want to touch him! You get over it, and get sticky too!

All the students were excited and laughing. I wasn't laughing! He was coming to me fast, wanting my help. I wanted to run from him! I told him to stop and not move another inch! He stopped. There was a glob of glue on his side of the table and a trail on the carpet leading to me.

I ran to get a bunch of paper towels, called the custodian, and took him to the nurse. She had extra clothes for accidents. We were not able to have reading that day.

It is my desire to inform parents, caregivers, and others about my experiences because they are typical of what happens in most elementary schools on any given day. Middle school and high schools have their own dynamics and are much more serious. The issues facing schools begin at home.

Becoming a better kindergarten teacher was my goal. I would not be able to say this if a devoted teacher, Ms. Lilly, hadn't taken me by the hand and shown me the most effective way to teach the little ones. Ms. Lilly would bring my class and me into her room and teach my kids and hers while I watched as she introduced the reading lesson and station activities.

When she felt I was comfortable, she watched as I instructed both groups. It was not an easy job to know how to reach, teach, and touch these little ones. I believe one has to have a certain something to teach them.

She has part-time help. "Granny" is a great help to Ms. Lilly. Ms. Lilly does meet the AYP standards with about 99 percent of her students. She may have one child that does not meet the standards. It wasn't because the teacher or the child had not tried.

Hurray for all the Alice's and Gloria's who go beyond the call of duty! They genuinely love the students.

Parents and caregivers please do not push your child into a higher grade if they have not met the criteria for that grade. That is a grave mistake. You are hurting them. Leave them there another year. Another year in that same grade can make a huge difference in behavior, self-esteem, and academic status. They need that extra year to mature—plus they already have experience and knowledge the others don't. They can become a leader.

Two years ago, while teaching kindergarten, there was a boy who had not been to school at all. His slate was clean. He hardly knew his name, could not recognize it when he saw it, and knew no letters in his name. I could see his frustration. The students didn't want to play with him. Some would snicker when it was his turn to read, write, and pronounce letters or numbers.

His eyes were always glossy with tears. He began to act out, doing and saying inappropriate things. I had formed somewhat of a bond with him and would take him aside to reassure him that he could learn to read and write. He had already given up.

It was imperative that I call his home; messages were left, and notes sent home by his older cousin. There was no response.

After a while another teacher came into the class. Upon seeing her, I would ask about him. He had gotten completely out of control. He was suspended and had to have Mom come to a meeting in order to bring him back to school. She came to the meeting.

It was suggested that he stay back another year. Ms. Lilly became his teacher. Wow! What a change! He was like a new boy. All the students liked him. He was reading, writing, and smiling.

I had a chance to substitute for Ms. Lilly and saw the huge changes. When he saw me, he ran up and gave me a big hug and a smile. He told me how well he was doing. What a difference another year makes.

The most productive way to prevent retention of a child is to prepare them academically and socially before entering school. At the onset of recognizing your child has challenges at school, get help from your friends and suggestions from the teacher. Please don't ignore it. Your child's future depends on it.

What kind of future will the child have? It's up to you! You are reading a book from a person who failed third grade. I didn't put forth the effort, so my mom suggested that I needed another year. I had a love for drawing. I was very good at it. I helped the teacher with the bulletin boards. Drawing was always on my mind. I faked studying and half-did my homework.

Staying back was the best thing that could have happened to me and was a lesson well learned. The teacher had done her part. There were no classroom distractions or disturbances that cut down on the teaching time.

I am grateful that Mom recognized the problem and took the proper action. My future depended on it. I don't believe I could have fulfilled my potential. I am still working on it. I am not even close to it.

I believe that God put these desires in my heart and will keep his promise. "Commit to the Lord whatever you (I) do and your (my) plans will succeed" (Prov. 16:3, NIV). "I remind you to stir up (use) the gift of God, which is in you. For God did not give us a spirit of fear but a spirit of power, of love and of a sound mind (self-discipline)" (2 Tim. 1:6-7, NIV).

We are not to be fearful or timid about what must be done because we love what we do. We discipline our children so they are prepared and ready! Let's do it!

Thinking I had completed the chapter on No Child Left Behind/ AYP, in February, 2013, I was rewarded with the opportunity to substitute in the class of my mentor, Mrs. Brown. These four year old preschool students remembered that I had taught them earlier in the school year. It was in October, 2012. What I encountered was a "WOW" experience!

What a difference four months made! The teacher assistant, students, and I left on a high note! They were excited to show me that their social behavior and academic skills had improved.

During the morning block when language, math, science and reading are taught, all were eager to show their recall of facts on the previous objectives. Their recall was astounding! I introduced *The Weekly Reader* article concerning President's Day and explained that was the reason they were not at school on Monday, February 19, 2013.

They were able to recall the first president, George Washington, the 16th president, Abraham Lincoln and the 44th, President Barak Obama! They were able to pronounce, precisely, each syllable in President Obama's name. Someone said, "and Sasha and Malia are their children's names." These students will certainly be ready for kindergarten!

Remembering the names of the presidents on the coins and bills was a 'no-brainer'! They learned something new. They learned that Abraham Lincoln's and George Washington's faces were among other presidents carved out of the mountain at Mount Rushmore.

There should be no reason for students not to know this information as they move to higher grades.

Permit me to go back to my day in Mrs. Brown's class. Not only had she taught the objectives, social behavior and character, she also had assistance and a low class size of eighteen students.

Please, let me not forget. The students showed manners and gratitude, saying, "please" and "thank you". My opinion is that they had been taught the behaviors at home and at school. Parental participation was evident; therefore, academic acceleration had occurred.

Before I finish this chapter, take another look at these precious four year old students. That day, I will never forget!

As they were seated on the carpet with legs crisscrossed, hands in their laps, their faces showed that they had been satisfied with the day. I continued to remind them how sweet they were and how proud I was with their behavior. I continued to remind them how smart they were, that I had not heard tattling, fussing, or fighting! Someone said, "You are so cute." Someone else said, "You are so smart!" Another said, "You are so handsome!" I heard, I love you," and responded, "Thank You, I love you all." The assistant, the students and I just laughed.

Here is an affirmation I made up which is repeated all during the day. They make hand movements as they say, "I'm smart! I can do this work! It's not too hard for me because I am **smart**!" By the way, this is repeated to every classroom I visit.

It was now time to go home. As we walked down the hall to meet their parent's, they could see the joy and peace on their faces. To see the light in their eyes, you know you have captured their hearts.

The capture of pre-kindergarten classes is being played out all over America on any given day. My question is . . . How would anyone NOT want this in every school? Our President and most Americans agree. Why not everyone? Not one of these students will be left behind; they will make Annual Yearly Progress!

Again, thanks to all of the teachers who make it happen in spite of the hardships, rejections, lack of finances and whatever else that comes up! Loving the children is what makes it happens!

Whose Responsibility Is It Anyway? Am I My Brother's Keeper?

We are our brother's keeper (Gen. 4:9, NIV), and we are to help our brother (Jos. 1:14, NIV). That includes all of us.

Thanks to technology, the world's news has brought us closer together. We know more about each other than ever before. The information coming across our airwaves enhances our businesses, homes, churches, and communities.

"We are our brother's keeper" shows that we can—and we certainly should—be responsible for each other on a worldwide basis.

I am aware that there are churches that are being responsible to others. However, my church, Faith Landmarks Ministries, provides food, furniture, clothes, and money to our members, to people in other cities, and to neighboring communities.

Our tithes and offerings support our community and countries in Africa, Asia, India, and South America on a yearly basis. We have schools, orphanages, and Bible institutes in some of these countries.

It is my desire to give you a picture of the wealth of support you can receive if you see and realize that many people seek to assist you. This guide will help you reach your goal; however, you must decide and commit. Begin with the end in mind. The end is the peaceful home, the reason for my writing this book. It has been inside me for about forty years.

I have taught thousands of students over these years and have stored inside myself many experiences, lessons, and successes. There were also some failures. The failures cause me to wish I had known more ways to help.

Some people said, "Pat, you're not God! You can't help every child!"

I realize that, but it hurts when I see them headed on the wrong path, which eventually ends in incarceration and death. "Discipline your son (daughter) for in that there is hope. Do not be a willing party to their death" (Prov. 19:18, NIV).

I realize that there are parents who did discipline their children, but they got mixed up with the wrong peer group and followed them instead of parental discipline. If they are not dead, there is still hope in prayer. Don't give up on them. Many parents can attest to the fact that prayer saved their sons and daughters who had gone astray. "And when he is old, he will not depart from it" (Prov. 22:6, NIV).

Our children should come from responsible, caring homes. They should be ready to learn in positive school environments and then enter society to fulfill their destinies with great potential.

This is not just pie-in-the-sky thinking. The truth is many families fit this bill. It is not impossible. Nothing will be impossible for you (Matt. 17:20, 19:26, Mark 10:27, NIV).

I am aware that for many parents—especially in single-parent homes—it is especially difficult. However, it is not impossible. On CoCo Brother's radio show, Pastor Dale Bonner said, "If just one person does it that knocks your excuse out of the water!" That's true because many times we hide behind excuses, limiting ourselves and our families.

Whose Responsibility Is It Anyway? Responsibility and Respect for Each Village

Responsibility means being able to respond in an appropriate manner. When we see and hear the myriad of unfortunate occurrences that have buffeted our children over the years, especially in the past two decades, we sometimes shake our heads and wonder whose responsibility it is.

Newspapers, magazines, and radios share unfortunate reports about our children. Much of the time, we blame each other for what is happening to our youth. We remain in our villages that are in need of real and lasting support while the majority of our youth continue to go rapidly downhill.

Over the years, some efforts have been successful. We can do more together on a larger scale to fix our education system. People in each state must join together in unity.

Education Nation has stepped up to the plate. Our nation needs to respond to our children and youth in an appropriate manner where success in education is concerned. www.EducationNation.com. It was reported that more than one million kids drop out of school each year. Can you fathom that? That number represents 7,000 a day! I hope you are alarmed. I believe you are thinking, "I have seen this information before." I did mention that I repeat certain things for emphasis.

Whose responsibility is it to make sure that most students remain in school? Experts agree that keeping our kids in school can save billions of dollars in health care and crime—and it will help prepare the next generation for jobs. It looks like each village must do its part to close that gap. I hope you are thinking about what you can do. It takes God and the whole village to raise our children from the grass up.

Again, after I thought I had concluded editing, the current news was replete with topics on education; preschool, special education, teacher lay-offs that affect the whole education system, as well as the other people who will lose their jobs. What I was reading caused me to look back at my chapters. Fourteen of the chapters had addressed the current issues facing our youngest to the oldest family members. Many topics were on closing/bridging the gaps, prevention/intervention with parental assistance at home, especially the first five years.

As I watched the Cycle MSNBC with Krystal Ball 2-15-13, the guest was Milton Chin, author of 'Education Nation' The ABC's of Success. His topic was on bridging/closing gaps, and educating the parents on how to teach their children at home. Mr. Chin says, "This will not add to the national debt, but will enhance it."

Secretary of Education, Arne Duncan discussed how to teach parents what to do. That is exactly what this guide does. He states that positive help from parents with our children in the first five years is what is needed. video.msnbc.msn/thecycle/50894042.

Last, but not least, President Obama, in his State of the Union and in subsequent addresses, proposed making "high quality preschool available to every child in America;" to make sure all children start life n an equal footing and also closing the education gap of our children beginning at home."

I cannot fathom in my head and heart who could not agree that ALL of God's children are our responsibility and that we should respect each village. When and if this is done, we will all reap the benefit of safer communities.

CNN's documentary, "Don't Fail Me Education in America," was reported by Soledad O'Brien on May 15, 2011, as she followed three high school students in a national robotics competition. Thousands of students competed. Only a small number made it to the finals: many finalists were Asian. The schools that won were middle-class schools.

The whole competition was based on character values. They won by building respect and responsibility for each other. That built confidence in each of them. When individuals have confidence and commitment, no one can stop or top them.

It has been said that there are no jobs out there. Secretary of Education Arne Duncan states that there are two million available jobs with high wages from high-profile employees. Coco Brother, of Radio Station 104.7, has also reported this repeatedly.

What's the problem? Why aren't these jobs being filled by our young black and white students? The Asians are filling most of these jobs because others are not qualified. Only 25 percent pass the high school's advanced placement classes. When Asian students come to our universities, they have been prepared at home before school. No nonsense!

Educational testing statistics have indicated that an increasingly high percentage of Asian students are very successful in math and science classes, even though they comprise a small percent of the nation's population. A generation ago, we used to be on top. Now the United States is ranked much lower in science 17 percent and math 25 percent because our children have lost their focus on learning. The focus on learning must become their highest priority again. However, it must begin at home. In my opinion, the answer lies in the last two sentences, which is the purpose for this guide. We must begin somewhere; therefore, home is the most logical place if we expect our education system to be competitive.

Many of our students have a misconception about what school is for. School is for learning—not partying, playing, disrespecting, fighting, bullying, or murdering. It must be stopped! We can do it together. I hate to think it will get worse. Whose responsibility is it to make it better for all children? Reread this again.

M. V. Lange on Education Nation September 2010, stated,

> "I don't believe education can be fixed until we begin to fix our families. When teachers are expected to teach children how to be decent citizens, there is no time to teach reading and math. We continue to throw money at schools and only see the problem getting worse. Maybe the money needs to go to educating the parents to discipline effectively. If teachers could get back to teaching instead of spending so much time trying to discipline and stop bad behavior, we would see much more success."

I turn to the Bible when I need answers. "Discipline your son (daughter) for in that there is hope; do not be a willing part to their death" (Prov. 19:18, NIV).

"Stop listening to instruction my son (daughter) and you will stray from the words of knowledge" (Prov. 19:27, NIV).

"Listen to advice and accept instruction and in the end you will be wise" (Prov. 19:28, NIV).

I don't expect children to read this book; however, it is my hope that you will use these scriptures as you guide them—if you are committed to change yourself first. Take another look at Goethe's couplet.

Let me *school* you on whose responsibility it is. With this book, I intended to uncover some things, ideas, and situations that have been around and accepted for years. The thinking seems to be, since we have always done it this way, it must be right. Hold up! Are ideas and situations right because they have been around for eons? They may seem right to us, but they may not be true or reliable.

Let us respond with our piece of the puzzle to make it one beautiful puzzle for all to see. With each additional puzzle piece, our children will excel more. Search your heart. Look for ways you can assist. Go and volunteer at your neighborhood school.

Recently, I was trying to recruit parents to help at school. A Hispanic mother whose son was in my class said, "Can I really come to school and help? I have wanted to ask, but I didn't know if I could!"

I said, "Go to the office and ask to volunteer."

She hugged me and held me, crying. So, I started to cry.

Then she said, "I could really help! Really?" She couldn't believe it.

Many people could volunteer. It could be an hour per day. Volunteer or just go sit beside your child, especially if problems exist. You could sit beside another child who has problems staying on task.

If you have a child who is in trouble at school, don't let him or her know you are coming. Just show up. Tell them you will pop in anytime. This will help them know you mean business. They will not continue to waste everyone's time.

Go by McDonald's and surprise them with a lunch when possible. You don't know how much this builds their self-esteem.

Some people don't have children, know any children, or like children! They might not know how to help. Visit the school to see if you can run copies for teachers. Grade some papers. Don't worry—they will give you an answer sheet. For the others, volunteer to sit beside a rambunctious child so they can stay focused. Work with the letters, sounds, counting, or printing.

You can use flash cards to help them remember and retain math and spelling skills. Each school has unique ways you can be of service.

For the ones who love children, there are numerous ways you could be of service. Become a Lunch Buddy. You should see the smiles from the Lunch Buddy adults and children. It is a wonder to behold! Become a Big Brother or a Big Sister. Enroll your children in the BBBS programs in your city.

Denzel Washington is spokesperson for the Boys and Girls Clubs of America. I read an article about how becoming a member turned his life around. Dr. Ben Carson's mother was single and kept her son off the streets by sending him to the Boys Club.

Don't forget about the YWCA and the YMCA. They have had similar successes with young people that turned their lives around.

Bridging the Gap

Part I: Behavior Management at Home

To make the biggest impact on our families, I am bringing school to your home. All caregivers can view some of the important issues that have impacted parents and teachers, how we have interacted with each other over the years, and how these actions have affected our children.

For many years, there has been a widening gap between our schools and homes. With *A Parent's Guide to a Peaceful Home*, I am attempting to bridge that gap. As you read this guide, you will discover that I am also including caring, responsible adults who love our children.

You will be surprised at the number of responsible adults, schools, and businesses that have interceded and are doing monumental things for our children. I am approaching the issue from a teacher's point of view.

Some parents think the teachers don't like their children. The teacher or school calls home on a number of occasions because of the child's behavior. These calls have occurred continually over a period of months or years.

There are very few teachers that do not like your child for no reason at all! There may be a few teachers that do not like your child because of race or ethnicity. I hope they are few and far between. The mistaken idea that some teachers don't like certain children has something else behind it. A child might say, "The teacher is picking on me. The teacher doesn't like me."

More than likely, the teacher had to speak to the child frequently because of disturbances and disruptions in class. The teacher is responsible for the safety and academic success of each child; distractions cut down on the instruction time. Teachers do not like the behavior—not the student. Some students say, "My teacher doesn't like me! She's always fussing at me and picking on me!"

I ask if are there any students in the class that the teacher never has to speak to. They usually name two or three students. I ask, "Do you know why?" When they don't readily come up with a reason, I ask about their behavior.

They say, "Mrs. James never fusses at Joseph. He always does his work and doesn't ever get in trouble!"

I say, "Why would the teacher fuss at him for no reason? Why would she fuss at Joseph?"

They had not processed the real reason. Take your child to school to discuss the reasons why this is occurring. You will help your child see that you will not condone bad behavior because the child is stopping the entire class from learning.

Badmouthing the school and the teacher builds resentment in the child. Your negative or positive attitude towards the teacher and the school reflects their actions at school.

These kinds of incidents should be nipped in the bud. If not, your child will perceive your actions as not caring about how they act. They won't care nor will they listen to the teacher anymore. A negative attitude toward the school and the teacher opens the door to lifelong problems. Be aware of what you are breeding. Mom used to say, "You may not make all A's, but you will behave!"

The child may end up dropping out of school mentally long before it occurs physically.

Introduce them to a love of learning before they enter school. Once you realize how to capture their attention to learning new things, you will be surprised by how they soak in so much information. They are like sponges. You will also see behavior changes.

A basic reason for inappropriate behavior is not being introduced to a love of learning and socialization. I am not as interested in teaching them how to read as I am in teaching them a love of learning. If they learn to love learning, it will not be difficult to teach them anything.

The lack of social skills makes a huge difference in how much they learn in the earlier years. Statistics say that 90-95 percent of their brains are formed by the age of four. This is a critical time to prepare children to learn, leave the nest, and go to daycare or preschool.

Some children leave home with a clean slate; almost nothing has been taught to them. That is where the problems begin. The child begins school with no skills. The child does not know how to sit still, be quiet, or keep his hands to himself.

Even a child is known by his actions by whether his conduct is pure or right. The actions of a child in his early years point to the direction his life is taking (Prov. 20:11, NIV).

Don't ignore or sweep bad behavior under the rug. You will be able to deal with them properly if you follow my suggestions. "Discipline your son (daughter) for in that there is hope" (Prov. 19:18). No discipline results in no hope.

In order to discipline your children properly, "Listen to advice and accept instruction and in the end you will be wise" (Prov. 19:20, NIV). You will end up with wise children. If we start them out right, they will most likely end up right. Know what you want. Go after it. Don't stop until you get there. "Two are better than one because they have a better return for their labor" (Eccl. 4:9, NIV).

"If one falls down, his friend (parent, brothers, sister) can help him (them) up: But pity the man (child) who falls and has no one to pick him up" (Eccl. 4:10, NIV).

The world is in crisis because many homes do not have a support system. Children are not getting the kind of nurturing they deserve. Some are growing up like weeds, but they don't know which way to grow. No clear boundaries have been set.

Peer pressure and bullying begin early in their lives. Many of their problems come from following their peers—even when they know they shouldn't. "Don't be misled, bad company corrupts good behavior" (1 Cor. 15:33, NIV).

He made me do it! She was doing it! He told me to take it! They told me to hit her! They gave me the answers.

Teachers have heard these excuses thousands of times. Far too many children are drawn to the ones who cause the most problems. Therefore, you have to be the one to teach right from wrong.

Bridging the Gap

Part II: Learning at Home

Are you truly committed and ready to seize the moment? If you are you, your children will be glad.

Here are some easy suggestions for learning at home. Point out common things around the house by colors. "Look at your green socks. Let's see how many green things you can find." Do this with all colors.

Do the same thing with numbers. "Let's count how many green things you found. Show me with your fingers how many green things you found." Make it exciting. Tell them they will earn a treat.

Fill a treasure box with Dollar Tree items. Let them earn a treasure for finding green things. They must use their manners and say, "Thank you." Hold on to it until they thank you.

"Show me with your fingers how many meatballs you want on your spaghetti. Tell me how many that is."

Use these techniques in their learning with common items as lessons. You are fostering a love for learning. Include siblings in these activities. Use every new experience as a teachable moment. Enlist older siblings to continue your effort to learn and earn.

When you are driving, point out different places by name because you want them to name them. Discuss the letter name sounds and colors of things and places they see.

Printing their names on their things will help them recognize their names. Teach them how to spell their names. Make up songs for the letters to their names.

Permit older ones siblings to earn bigger things like burgers or popcorn so they get the connection between learning, teaching, cooperation and earning. Make a big deal out of each person involved in the process.

I use this activity at schools to get them to complete their work. Use the TV and computer as learning tools—not just to play games. The games should be a reward they earn. By using the computer as a learning tool, they will learn their letters, sounds, colors, and how to count. Many school districts have reading, math, science and social studies work on the computer. Ask your child's teacher for other websites to enhance learning.

Use the public library. It helps to get out of the house. It also cuts down on purchasing books, CDs, and DVDs and the use of their computers. Put the library schedule on a calendar. I rediscovered the library while writing my book. Writing at home caused me to become too comfortable. A myriad of things kept me from making writing a priority. It's not hard to become distracted at home. Life happened! I did not stick to the schedule I had set for myself for writing. It was easy to let time slip away.

I prayed, "Lord, You become my Master Scheduler. Help me organize myself. I know You gave me the privilege to be a writer and to do what is necessary to finish the book, so that the parents and their children can have a guide that will benefit them and their children's children."

"Because God is the author and finisher of my faith, He impressed upon me that my tongue is the pen of a skillful writer" (Heb. 12:12, NIV).

Although I was not yet convinced, I obeyed. I went to the library at the scheduled times and gained confidence each day I visited. I was able to finish the book. I pray that you will internalize the message . . . **You have to do something different if you want a different result**.

The Bible has answers for all of my problems. When I tried to engage in other projects or change careers, it took me years to realize that I had traveled this same road. It took a big leap of faith to trust Him and not lean on my own understanding (Prov. 3:5, NIV).

I become energized when I find scriptures to fit my problems and internalize them. I also receive more faith and strength. Finding scriptures causes me to know that the Lord is leading me as the author and finisher of my faith (Heb. 12:2, NIV). "My people shall dwell in a peaceful habitation (house) and in secure dwellings and in quiet resting places" (Isa. 32:18, NIV).

God wants our homes to be peaceful and we should have quiet resting places for our families. I believe you want that too. As you take steps in that direction, you will get enough strength and faith to finish the course. God will also lead you as you guide your family. You have faith because you will have listened to the Word of God.

Do you want your children to love reading? I know you do. You wouldn't even think of saying, "No". You go first. Let them see you reading instead of looking at the television during all of your spare time. *What does she mean by spare time? I don't have any spare time!* Oh, but you do! Do you watch television at all? Do your children see you watching television on a regular basis? It is about what you prioritize.

Have no-one-watches-television days, especially on school days. Your children will think you have lost your mind! With all of the fun and learning activities going on, they won't even miss the TV. The weekend will become TV time.

Ask older siblings to assist them in becoming better readers and learners. Reward the older siblings for their help. Find out what they want and like. You can work it out.

Find 3 x 5 cards for the older siblings. Write, print, and tape the names on the objects. Leave them there for a while. You decide how long.

Everyone should get in the game. Point out what the names represent. You are testing them, but they don't know it yet. Take it off the object. Say the name. Ask them to put the card back where it was while naming and spelling it.

Don't be embarrassed if people come by and wonder why the table, door, and chairs have cards taped to them. Explain and show off your children as you take each one off. Let the little ones put them back in the proper place. After a while, they will learn to spell, say, and write them. Select a day to test them but don't call it a test. Let them know they will get a treat for saying and putting them back in the right place. Your friends will go home and do the same thing. We don't want anyone to outdo us. A little competition won't hurt.

Do you want them to be speedy, fluent readers? I know you do! For the little ones, use their books. Dr. Seuss's books are full of creatures with nonsense rhyming words. Let's not forget the wonderful illustrations.

They can take those books and read them while the words are upside down. They will learn to read them right side up!

You can teach fluent reading by "shadow reading." Take the book. Read one word. Have them read that word. Read the next word. Let them read that word after you. Go back and read word one and two together. They will also read words one and two. Repeat this procedure for an entire sentence. They should read the sentence. After a while, they will be able to shadow read an entire paragraph for other siblings. Reward them whenever they make an attempt to assist. Make sure you read and pause at commas. Stop completely at the end of sentences. Raise your voice when you come to an exclamation point or when you read a question.

For comprehension, ask them who, what, when, where, why, and how questions after each sentence. When they come to the end of the paragraph, ask them to tell you what that paragraph was about. Remind them to use who, what, when, where, why, and how answers.

You will learn how to structure the questions to the ages of the children. Ask the little ones to name the animal and ask them to tell where the animal is located.

This exercise will also be used by all of the older siblings. They will be able to write, on the margins of tests and on all worksheets, the six types of questions. Wherever I teach, I use these exercises. I ask, "Would you rather have 65 percent or 100 percent on each test you take?"

I remind them that they have the capacity to get 100 percent. That is the goal. I tell them to put 100 percent on the corner of every paper the teacher gives them. It's their goal. It reminds them that they are going to scratch up, mark up and mess up that paper by writing who, what, when, where, why, and how near the six question words. They may write them in the margins and draw arrows to the question words. Circle the important words. They may draw pictures in the margins to remind them what the paragraph was about.

They must take special note of italicized and bold words, use context clues, and look at the sentences above, beneath, and surrounding the important words. Write the definition over the word or in the margins. Boldfaced and italicized words will probably be asked about on the test.

Many times, they are allowed to highlight important sentences or words. If they are not taught what to highlight, they will most likely highlight the whole paragraph.

Each paragraph should be blocked off or underlined and numbered. On the test, they should refer to the paragraph's numbers to answer questions. Sometimes they are numbered, but sometimes they are not. When they finish reading and following these instructions, they understand what the passage means—and they are ready for the test.

I have a few test-taking skills for them to remember. There are usually four questions. They should read all four. There are two answers that are detractors. First look for the one that makes no sense at all. Scratch that one out. Look at the next answer. There may be a word that says "never" or "always." Scratch that one out. When they are down to two answer choices, they have a 50 percent chance to get it right. Look in the margins and at the notes—the answer may be on the page. It could be a grammar question that had nothing to do with the test. That's why they must pay attention during instruction.

Another test-taking skill for unanswered questions may come down to a process of elimination. The correct answer may be the first thought they have. Have you ever taken a test and realized when you got the test back that the one you scratched out was the correct answer? If you are not 100 percent sure, stick with the first thought. Many tests will have the answers stated in a slightly different way later on in the test.

Do not leave any questions unanswered. That will count against you. Answer all of the questions using the skills you have learned.

These test-taking skills are not just for children. Mom, if you are going back to school, these tips will benefit you. Knowing how to take tests will alleviate the fear associated with taking tests. Look back at how much fun you had learning new things. Did you notice there was no fear—just fun? Learning can be like that if you approach it in a fun way.

They will be ready for school when you prepare them properly. Remember the 90-95 percent window of opportunity that the young children have? You close the gap when you do these exercises with your children.

At one school, the math specialist said, "I'm so glad I saw you. I want you to know you are responsible for my students making 600 on the year-end test. She said they did what you taught them when you substituted."

When I visit schools, many students tell me the same thing.

Before I close this chapter, I must reiterate the importance of building character at home. That will close a huge gap that has existed for generations. Character training should be taught at home because many school districts do not have a successful character program in place. If parents teach character at home, teachers can educate, teach, and instruct at school.

The Bible says, "Train up your child." Parents train. Teachers teach. If this was happening on a wider scale, teachers could use the instructional time to teach instead of training and disciplining.

By the time we get through training, there are a few pitiful minutes left to teach. Teachers must make sure the students make AYP and that no children are left behind! Why aren't the teachers teaching? Training absorbs the majority of the time—not instructing.

I was given a notepad that described the duties of a teacher. Each of the one hundred job descriptions fit the tasks teachers attempt to complete daily. Thank God we don't have to wear all one hundred of those hats every day! A teacher is a mediator, lawyer, doctor, nurse, judge, nurturer, peacemaker, and god, seeing everything and being everywhere at the same time. He/she must be omnipotent and omnipresent; have all power to settle every dispute that sometimes occurs at home, on the bus, at lunch time, at recess. In other words, teachers know all the answers to all the dilemmas and how to solve them: Omniscient, having the capability to make sure that every child passes every test all the time, even when every child is not listening, not following directions, and causing disruptions; but make sure that all children make AYP and that no child is left behind. Oh, I forgot one important one: a teacher is a magician.

I hope I have not discouraged any prospective teachers. If you love children and have a passion for teaching, then come on in! You are needed! At least you know more than what was taught in the teaching methods book you had to pass in college. I am not saying methods classes are not needed. You need to know the methods; however, you need some realistic experience so that you don't run out of the building during student teaching and never return.

If you don't have—or have lost—exuberance or passion for teaching, think about other options. I have many friends who are looking forward to retirement for this reason.

Let God direct your next steps. You don't want to work and worry yourself to death. This has happened to many teachers who were also parents.

I am confident that because you have more information on what to do and how to train children, you will get them ready to enter school so that they can make AYP. You will have closed the gap; your child will not be left behind. It needs to start at home.

The Family Meeting

Part I: Stand Tall and Set Your Parameters

What's so important about family meetings? I have heard about it in almost every chapter.

The family meeting is the backbone for building a peaceful, loving home. Without it, there would be no need to read this book. It is the lifeblood, the glue that will bring success to each member of the family.

That's a tall order. Can there be any such thing?

It is a tall order, but it can be done. There are families who have had a transformation at home because they all bought into initiating family meetings. They know what to expect and what the consequences will be. No surprises. No excuses.

They know where the boundaries are, what the rules are, and when to stop. There is no fear of physical, mental, or sexual abuse from family members. Their homes are safe havens where they feel valued.

When I see former students they greet me with a big hug and a big smile. I inquire about how they are doing at home and at school. The students and the parents have positive reports. I have an inner feeling that they are telling the truth. No one is looking down. We have direct eye contact.

The goal of the family meeting is to teach discipline. This will bring unity to the home. You have read this before, but it is worth repeating. If a house is divided against itself, it cannot stand (Mark 3:25, NIV).

If there is no structure and everyone is going in their own direction, it erodes to the point of collapsing. Only you know how bad it is. *I can't take it anymore! I don't know what else to do!*

Henry David Thoreau said, "Go confidently in the direction of your dream." Put that vision in the front of your mind. Go for it!

A peaceful home will be yours quicker than you think. This happens when all family members see that they are valued, have a voice, have a place, fill a space, have worth, have peace, and have their needs met. Think about the major building blocks you will have erected for them. What a legacy you will have left for them and the next generation!

What you do for them now will become the legacy for their children's children. A good man leaves an inheritance for his children's children (Ps. 13:22, NIV).

One generation will command your works to another; they will tell of your mighty acts (Ps. 145:4, NIV).

You are about to enter the family meeting zone. Be reminded that, without the family meeting, you will have what you always had. You know whether your home is one of peace or one coming to pieces.

Remember Goethe's couplet? Only you can become committed. Allow your children to see their new transformed teacher in you. Go ahead—you can do it!

The Family Meeting

Part II: Watch What You Say!

You have the floor! Stand tall and watch what you say!

When I was a child, I used to hear, "Sticks and stones will break my bones, but words can never harm me." We all know that is not true. Sticks and stones can break your bones—and words can certainly harm you.

Words used as weapons have caused much grief and death. The tongue has the power of life and death and those who love it will eat its fruit (Prov. 18:21, NIV). That includes all of us. No one is excluded. Some deaths have been physical and some mental.

Take a look at your life and recall the hurtful words that others have said to you. Some of those people were hurt by you. Have you gotten over them yet? Those people you hurt with your words may not have forgotten either.

I remember the pain and hurt that words have caused me. I have always thought of what I almost said in anger. On my way home, I would say to myself, "I should have said this or that and let them have a piece of my mind. The next time they say that to me, I'm going to tell them off."

However, there was never a next time. The pain and hurt took a long time to heal. I had to continually pray that I could forgive. Sometimes a small voice said, "Don't you say anything! I will work it out. I will restore you." He does restore.

Speaking loving words is always the right thing to do. I must remind parents that you are your child's first teacher, but now you have learned a more excellent way to conduct your houses. You have the floor. Call your first family meeting. Your demeanor must be one of authority sprinkled with lots of love.

Set your rules first. Let them know that what you see today is how this house will be run from now on. "Guess what? You will love it." Inform them how the improper use of computers and cell phones, and social media has devastated many homes across the world. "My hope is that you all do not want to hurt people, do you?"

Watch for feelings that surface. Discuss their feelings in the way you know how as a parent. Permit them to have a voice. Ask an older sibling to record the opinions. Have the recorder place the names beside their comment. Date it.

Make the meeting count. Tell them that their comments will be read at the next meeting. This causes them to know their ideas are important. If there is no one to record, it's your job. Recording the meetings solidifies the remarks. They are for reference—if and when there is a discrepancy. The recording gives the family meeting significance.

Be vigilant about checking to see where your children are surfing on the Internet. Let them know that you will be making regular "spy checks" so there are no surprises. Set a plan that you will follow if your child breaks a rule. The rule must be set in stone. Choose a punishment that will make them not to do it again.

Fussing doesn't work. It only makes them angry—and they have learned nothing. When you fuss, you say things you can't take back.

If you have teenagers or young adults who have a laptop, they need to know the rules are also for them. Even if the young adult bought their own computer and they remind you of that, let them know they are using your electricity!

If you find they have broken the computer rules, call a family meeting where all are present. Pull out the rules you set, select one of them, and read everything—including the date and the names of the family members who were present.

Say, "What is in these rules that you don't or didn't understand?" Express to them that you set the rules and the consequences—and you will carry out the punishment. There is no discussion at that time!

If they get feisty and disrespectful, remind them who you are and who they are. Ask them a few questions that will require them to think. Ask them, "Who pays the bills?" Wait for each answer. "Who pays the mortgage?" "Are you contributing to the finances?" Remind them they are consumers. "Do you buy your own clothes?" "You're a consumer!" "Do you buy food for the household?" "You consume the food!"

You are showing tough love. Do this without raising your voice. This is the time to discuss why the rule was broken?

Set the punishment. Remember it must hurt. You must take something away from them that hurts. You will know what hurts. Whatever it is, let them know how long the punishment will be. Please do not give in or give up. Use the incident to reinforce the rules for everyone.

You will need a recorder for each meeting. You can see how beneficial it is to be able to read verbatim the previous meeting. This solidifies the meetings.

Two incidents surrounding the computer in a home that could have caused serious damage to two teenage females are good examples.

Social media could have been very damaging to the girls if their parents had not stepped in immediately. Meetings were held to get to the bottom of it, and both incidents were resolved. Both cases involved boys. The oldest girl met her first interest through an introduction from a friend. They began talking on the phone, e-mailing, and using Facebook.

Almost as soon as she began communicating with him, she found out he had a child. The mother called repeatedly—even late at night—and brought the baby to the girl's basketball practice. Immediately she told the boy not to call her again. The calls did not stop from the mother or the father.

The Facebook connections continued as if there were a relationship. The baby's mother finally threatened to come to her house and cause bodily harm. This was done by phone and Facebook.

She threatened to go to her school to harm her and would not believe that once the teenager discovered that there was a child involved, that she had asked the boy not to call her anymore. Her parent called the police to have the girl arrested. They had lifted a threat from Facebook. The school had assigned persons to watch the teenager during the school day. She was summoned to court. This incident lasted about three months.

The great thing about this was the family support through the ordeal. There were meetings in which the family discussed the situation and how it would be resolved without any harm to either of the females.

The other incident involved a sixteen-year-old female. Someone sent her a text message about a very damaging Twitter message that was being circulated on the internet.

The grandmother heard about it after a meeting had adjourned. She asked what was going on, and was told that a boy had posted on Twitter that his friend had told him he had sex with the girl. She was upset—but not as upset as her teenager's mother. She was livid! The girl's father had also talked with her about it. She was not yet dating.

They all knew it was untrue, but what would the Twitter world think? The girl's mother called the person who initiated the Tweet, the pastor and assistant pastor to relay the message.

Both said, "Don't worry. We will take care of it."

They did. They lifted the message from Twitter and faced him with it. He profusely apologized over and over again. He said he was angry with his friend when he wrote it.

The girl's mother called him. He said he was sorry. She told him it was a little late to apologize. "Think about the damage you have done."

He said that he had a sister and a mother and wouldn't want anyone to say bad things about them.

His friend said he did not tell him that. He said anyone who knew the girl would not believe it.

The mother said that everyone does not know her daughter, and the damage was done. She saw the boy who posted the damaging message at church. He came up to her with his head down and confessed about how sorry he was.

Surprisingly, she reached out to him. He fell into her arms, crying profusely. She patted him on the back and said, "It's going to be okay." As she was comforting him, she thought, *"What are you doing? You're supposed to be mad! This Christian thing is no joke! He'd better be glad I've been a Christian more than two days!"*

He will never forget the mother who forgave him after he hurt her daughter. "A man's steps are directed by the Lord, how then can a man understand his (her) own way" (Prov. 20:24, NIV).

That is why the girl's mother embraced and comforted the very person who had hurt her daughter. She, on her own, would not have done it. That's the power of the Word coming through the spirit. We have to live it.

When the sixteen-year-old went to church, her friends said, "We didn't believe it anyway." She acts as though nothing happened. It didn't change her demeanor at all.

Both of these incidents could have been very damaging had Mom and Dad not kept a pulse on the situation to see that they were resolved properly. Their relationship is solid.

If parents would check, make the proper adjustments, and discuss issues before they get out of hand, we would not have all these horrifying statistics. We must stop being too busy to check on our children.

We are the adults. They are the children. They need to be taught boundaries right after birth. If this is done early, we will not see our children on the trash heap. They will be on top of the mountain, reaching their potential.

Check on your children often—and not just about computers. They must know you will be checking on everyday matters. Children and youth are not always honest. Not all adults are honest all the time, but children need guidance. Check, so things can be easily corrected—and no one will be hurt beyond repair.

Over the years, I have had parents say, "I trust my child, and my child doesn't lie." They will if they think it will keep them out of trouble. Let that trust grow as they prove they are trustworthy.

The Family Meeting

Part III: Action Steps and Strategies

Strategy I

The action steps and strategies you must follow closely to help your children reach their potential.

Step 1: Call a family meeting and discuss the purpose of the meeting:

- TEAM means Together Each Achieves More
- Unit means one
- To become a TEAM/Unit

- Begin the family meeting by praising each child (see 95 Ways to Praise in Appendix).
- Think of something unique about them.
- Form a circle, put each one in the circle, and praise them (Positive Bombardment).
- Do this once a week.
- Choose a different child each week.
- Tell them they need to show some character traits so that all recognize some extra effort on their part (for a healthy self-concept).
- Help your children to learn the poem "I Am Somebody" (see Appendix).
- The next time you do Positive Bombardment, each person has to say something positive about the sibling in the center. Mom, you must take a turn in the middle. You should hear many kind words of appreciation.

- Remind them that they are becoming a TEAM/Unit, and they are sharing and showing love for each other.
- Conduct the Family Meeting in a formal way. There are ideas throughout this guide.
- Use a composition book to record discussions that will be read at the next meeting and referenced when necessary.
- Make sure you have recorded the home rules. They need to see that you are serious. They know you took time to think about the home rules. Post a shorter version in a place where they can see them.
- After reading the rules, ask them for comments.
- Listen carefully to any discussions or suggestions. You may change or add their suggestions, but the rules are set in stone. They are crucial to the safety of the family, chores at home, homework, or other responsibilities.
- The character values are crucial. Boundaries are crucial.
- Listen for suggestions of fun things the family can do that do not cost money (picnicking at the park).
- Discuss the **Character Chart**, the **Calendar**, the **Think Sheet**, and the **Job Chart**. Show them how they will be used. Post them where they can be seen.**(See Appendixes IX-XII)**
- Have a Friday night reward fun and video night.
- Get some gifts and certificates from a dollar store and present them to the deserving children.
- Zero in on behavior, study habits, homework, spelling, math, reading, social science, and science grades. Your children should not have to wait for the teacher to do it at school.
- Discuss each of the expectations using the character chart and calendar. Get feedback so that they know exactly what is expected at home.
- Relate study habits and homework back to the chart.
- Remind them that you or an older sibling will be checking the backpack daily. Select a place to leave the backpack. If they don't leave it in the proper place, you or someone else should change the color on the chart.
- Select a place where each person studies. Some stores have individual lap desks that have places for books, papers, and cup holders.

- Older siblings should help the younger ones with homework. Tell them they are the teachers. Homework should be signed or initialed. Allow the older sibling to sign or initial the homework. Think about what a boost of confidence this brings to the sibling, realizing that they are trusted in such a way. They know that you really trust them. Inform the teacher of this situation.

I was blown away at the amount of reading, math, science and social science that is taught in kindergarten. Since I have taught all grades, I know the objectives that each student is expected to master. However, many have not learned them because of continuous disruptions that cut each subject short.

Sometimes when I hand them a test that the teacher left, they say, "Ms. Braxton, my teacher didn't teach me that."

I say, "Unless you missed a boatload of days, I know these objectives were introduced in preschool and kindergarten. What have you been doing? You are in the fifth grade. The presidents were introduced and taught to you in preschool and kindergarten."

Many times they will try to argue with me. "No, my teacher did not teach me that."

I say, "None of your teachers in first, second, third, or fourth grade taught that objective? I will discuss this with your teacher when I see her."

The reason behind this discourse is to remind you of the necessity to review each homework assignment because it needs repetition.

I was also blown away by the interactive notebooks that have objectives, colored, glued, drawn, and written for each subject. Discuss these strategies in your meetings. Tie them to the Character Chart and Calendar. This must be done at home if you want your children to succeed.

The Family Meeting

Part III: Action Steps and Strategies

Strategy II

Help Your Child Reach His or Her Potential
Step II: Character/Discipline Chart

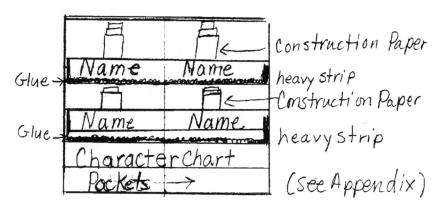

- Make a character chart (see Appendix XI).
- Find a colorful folder.
- Cut green, yellow, orange, and red construction paper to the size of a business card.
- Cut two strips of heavy paper. Glue them at the sides and the bottom of the strip. You need the top opened in order to stick the four business cards at the top of the strip.
- Stack them in the order of green, yellow, orange, and red over each name. The four strips represent the number of chances they get per day. The strips may be used to represent one chance per day.

- Use the strips to teach responsibility to whatever you deem they must not forget (chores, homework, putting the backpack by the door at night, and cleaning the bedroom).
- The colors will change from green to red as your child shows positive or negative behavior at home, school, and church.
- Remove the green and put it at the back at each rule infraction.
- I strongly suggest that you not fuss at them.
- They have to know they have stepped out of bounds and have to suffer the consequences.
- If you see disrespect in any form, remove the card to another color.
- Refuse to do anything special for them.
- You are following the rules you set up at the family meeting.
- The things they put on the calendar will have to wait until you see a positive change.
- I call the calendar "Fuss Buster." No one is allowed to fuss.
- Your child/children will link negative behavior with rewards lost and positive behavior will rewards earned.

If parents follow this guide and discipline their children at home, we could have much more success. The minor cost to them would be the cost of this guide, some dollar store items, and lots of meetings. It will unite them as a loving, peaceful family that has been taught discipline at home.

Strategy III

- Buy a **Job Chart** (See Appendix XI) for your children and laminate it. List their chores on this chart. This also may be purchased at a dollar store.
- Use stickers or markers to indicate when they have completed their chores. Rewarding with stickers is something they always like.

**Towards Affective Development Program
At-Home Tips to be Used in Conjunction with
Character Chart**

1. Behavior Change (+) (-)
   A. Impacts grades (+) (-)
      1. (+) Behavior = Rewards
      2. (-) Behavior = Family Meeting
         a. Set Rules
2. Refuse to buy them ANYTHING until behavior is (+) and they are on Green!
3. Calendar (see Appendix VIII)
   On the back of calendar, have children make a list of things they would like to do or have. Set dates when they may be able to do these things. Of course, it's dependent on whether they have fulfilled their responsibilities at school and home.
4. Refuse to buy them anything new until there is a (+) behavior change at home and school.

Note:
Together we can help _____(Child's Name)_____ get better in all areas. We become a team.

<u>T</u>ogether
<u>E</u>ach
<u>A</u>chieves
<u>M</u>ore

Mrs. Patricia Braxton
1/19/10

Most of the charts and graphs were created in my mind. That's what teachers do. My granddaughter, Paris, took pictures of my charts and graphs for this publication. I did not want to get them done professionally because it was important for you to see that you can make your own, and also create others that will fit your home situations and issues.

Strategy IV

Help Your Child Reach His or Her Potential
with a Parent Emergency Pack

As you read this you will recall the mother who successfully used this strategy with her daughter. This pack is probably the hardest, but also the best thing you can do to help your child become the best student and reach their potential.

This is tough love! Remember you are not to fuss with them. Just let them know at the initial meeting and subsequent ones that this peaceful home will be beneficial for everyone.

When their card is on red at home and school, the date we put on the Fuss Buster Calendar will have to wait until they can keep the card on green. The rest of the family will do what is on the Calendar. The child will spend the day or evening with Aunt Sue. They will not watch TV or use the computer.

"I have a few of your favorite books. I hope you will enjoy them. We will pick you up when we return."

Make sure you tell them what's going to be in the Emergency Pack. It must be something simple like a sandwich or two, soup, chips, and a drink or two.

"Don't ask Aunt Sue for anything to eat. You have your Emergency Pack!"

Remind the child of the good behavior you expect so they can go the next time.

"Of course, I know you're going to stay on green, aren't you?"

Every time the child gets on red, repeat the process. Don't get tired and quit! Those little stinkers or big stinkers are good at wearing parents down so they can "have their cake and eat it too!"

When you return, blow it up big! Come in as professional actors and actresses. This is the time to get loud, laughing and talking about the wonderful time you all had.

One way to stop negative behavior is to find something that really hurts. They will be thinking about how not following directions can hurt. And you don't have to fuss once.

I can guarantee that the child will come around soon. You are teaching them to become TEAM players. You are becoming a unit, and peace is at the door. Responsibility, respect, integrity, compassion, and trust are waiting in line.

As you continue the family meetings, these virtues will become a part of them. The children will learn boundaries. The little ones will be developing into responsible teenagers. The teenagers will transform as they watch you go first. That is what TAD/Towards Affective Development is about . . . Youth affecting change from within.

"If Mom can change—so can we."

Action Steps for the Family Meeting

- First, have your own Awards Ceremony. Then find games and videos that are appropriate for everyone. Make a big deal out of Friday Nights.
- Set a meeting time when all are there.
- Read the minutes.
- Always record the meeting. Someone needs to be the recorder.
- Discuss the first meeting.
- You want all of them to participate.
- Ask them their feelings about the first meeting.
- What did they like? What did they dislike?
- What do they think should be changed?
- What can they do to make things better?
- Does the **Think Sheet** help?
- Have they learned anything new?
- Do they feel better about how the house is being run?
- Discuss the **Character Chart**. Who stayed on green? Who got on red?
- Did they enjoy the **Calendar** event?
- How did they feel about not being able to participate in the **Calendar** events?
- Come up with additional questions.
- Read and discuss the **Contract** that must be signed by all.
- Discuss what they think about the **Contract.**
- Discuss time to Drop Everything and Read (DEAR). Everyone reads. TV and computers are all turned off.
- Discuss the books at the next meeting.
- Set a time for daily reading (fifteen minutes).

Formal Education, Skills, Gifts, and Talents

"Get an education. Get an education. We are preparing you for college!" I said this to my students at least two times a day, especially when I saw them goofing off.

However, the closer I came to retirement, the more I realized that every child might not be able, financially or academically, to go to college. What about those students? There are more of them who are not formally educated.

Take notice of each of your children in their early elementary years. Look at what they love to do. What do they have a passion for? You can use what they love to do as a catalyst to teach them discipline, responsibility, respect for themselves, respect for their siblings, and respect for others. Is it drawing, writing, technology, reading, talking, love of animals, building, or tearing things apart and putting them back together? If you have more than one child, you will need to keep a close eye and write it down.

This is a good reason to have a meeting. Surprise them with the written notes you have noticed about what they like to do. Discuss their likes with each one. You are pointing them in the right direction by acknowledging that you will let each of them do some special things pertaining to what they like. This excludes spending money. You will come up with unique ways to celebrate them through what they love.

Here are some matchless ways to entice all of them, even the tiniest, to learn the importance of money. This will also teach them that 'money doesn't grow on trees,' but it can grow if they keep adding to the pile.

I can hear you thinking. "Is she crazy? How can that be with this economy? How are they supposed to earn money at home?" Ok. Let's start little. Little can grow into much.

Inform them that they will be saving the money for bank accounts; savings, tithes, mad money to buy some things they want. I can hear them now. "Mom! Dad! When can we go to a dollar store?" I can see the pride on their faces as they go to the bank to open up their bank accounts and then head over to shop to get their items. I suggest that they get in the line and pay for the items they **earned.**

Use piggy banks first. They can be purchased at the dollar store. After the piggy banks are filled, use large jars with lids. They can decorate them with stickers and permanent markers. As you already know, the banks will have to be labeled with their names.

I have noticed, at most schools, that many children and teenagers are not interested in pennies and sometimes even nickels. I see pennies on the classroom floor, the playground, and the parking lot. I think they don't think of these coins as money. They won't pick them up. Well, let's change that. Parents, I'll bet you have pennies, nickels and even dimes that you could use to interest them to become collectors of the small stuff.

Why not get other family members, grandparents, aunts, uncles and friend involved as collectors of coins. Let them know about your new project. I'll bet they will be able to think of ways for your children to *earn* coins.

I say emphatically, "Stop giving them everything they want!" Begin to attach the word "**EARN**" to as many items as come to your mind. I will give you some strategies.

At the beginning, it is very important that you impress upon them that stealing others' earnings will cost them a lot! Whatever consequence you come up with for the pilferers must be very harsh! Remember. Don't fuss at them.

Now is the time for a Family Meeting. Look as stern as you can. Show them that this incident really hurt you. If you can, muster up a tear or two. Get out the tissue. Wipe your eyes and your nose. Sternly tell them the purpose for the called meeting. As you look at them, I'll bet you will see some tears and looking for tissues. You come up with the punishment. It must hurt them. They need to fill out the **Think Sheet**, go to red on the **Character Chart** and miss their **Calendar** date. Don't forget the **Emergency Pack!**

You may want to take the others on an extended date and leave the perpetrator with Aunt Sue. Just kidding! You get the point. At this point, I have just gone back to my childhood. Mom was wise enough to force me to see that stealing wasn't a fun thing to do.

You have probably noticed that I tell true stories that match the incidences of which I have written without naming them except in the cases where I was given permission. For this reason, I will tell this story as briefly as I can in a bare-bones manner.

In one of the states in which I taught, there was a young student who had a bad habit of taking everything that wasn't nailed down.

Of course, I notified his mother, however the stealing continued. Conferencing with him brought tears and apologies. He moved on up through to high school magnifying the habit. I remember having told him that it would end in jail, prison and or death. That habit finally led him to break into an apartment that he thought was empty, however, he was wrong. In order to stop the screaming person he took that person's life and prison became his home. This is just one story. There are many more.

I added this paragraph to admonish parents and caregivers to address the problem at the first sign of stealing. It's up to the adults to take proper steps when necessary. Here are some strategies to get you started.

Let them know that they can **earn** money even as they learn obedience; doing homework, following directions, staying on green on the **Character Chart**, doing chores, helping siblings to do the same. You will come up with more.

Look back at the chapters on ***Home Before School: Parts I, II, III and Taking School Home.*** Here is an example. Starting with the tots, use ideas such as, "Tell me how many meat balls are on your plate?" Reward them with the correct amount of pennies per meatballs.

I feel a cautionary word is needed here. You as a parent should know when you can permit them to handle coins without putting them in their mouths.

Another idea is to build character values as you tie them to positive behavior; RAKs (Random Acts of Kindness) at home, school, other family members homes, church, and in the community. Watch them. They will be running over each other (in a thoughtful way) trying to **earn** coins! You have read these words. 'Act the way you want to be and soon you'll be the way you act.' Who knows? You might see a bank president growing out of your effort. You can't lose!

Think about what you will have taught them. You have taught them how to **earn** money for what they want, which is an invaluable life lesson. You have taught them character values with giving hearts and attitudes of gratitude. These action steps will enhance their gifts and talents whether they will have formal training or not' their potential will be limitless and it all started with **earning** the little stuff.

Let them draw pictures and color them. Post them. Paste them. Glue them. Do whatever you have to do to show off their skills. Take them to the library to get books, CDs, and DVDs pertaining to their passion. At the next meeting, have them show their art or writing and discuss what they liked about the book, CD, or DVD. Let the teacher know of their special interest and ask for help with other ideas. Look for library books about their special talents or skills.

Most schools in America focus on writing each morning or some mornings. Others have at least one day of free writing. This is time to write, draw, and report on their talents. Many teachers permit their children to read, write, or draw when their work is complete. Let your little ones know that you want a copy of what they drew or wrote about. That means they have to do it two times—one for school and one for home.

Students need a folder for their work to enable them to show responsibility for keeping it. If you are exhibiting respect for their work, others will also respect it. You will be able to use the home meetings to show off their work to Grandma, Grandpa, Auntie, and friends.

With this paradigm shift in your own thinking, you will create new and better ways to promote respect, responsibility, caring, sharing, and discipline. You will not have to fuss with them. They are doing what they want—and you are getting what you want.

Television and computers are off limits at these times. After a while, they will forget about TV. You can let them find pictures on the computer for printing and discussion during the meetings. They will become more creative and confident, and will be empowered to seek that for which they have a passion.

This takes me back to acquiring a formal education. These creative activities are building skills they will love and experience regularly. Interviewers always ask, "What experience do you have?" They will be able to speak with fervor about the skills they have acquired. When your child seeks employment in the area of their experience, they will be able to showcase their skills and talents when they get that job and move up the ladder rapidly. They can build their own business from these experiences and become managers more quickly. The possibilities are endless.

As far as money is concerned, they will earn more money than their teachers. That's really not hard to do without a formal education. I will get on a bandwagon for a second. The reason almost everyone has a job, education, or business is because of teachers.

Many Amish children don't go past eighth grade, yet they learn to build communities that benefit all who live in or visit these communities.

Frederick Douglas was a proponent for teaching our children skills for life through the use of industrial education schools. He wanted them to use their gifts and talents to enhance their lives, communities, and futures.

If you use these examples, you will have structured a new, different relationship with your children. Your home will be noticeably more pleasant. Peace will burst out all over! "Discipline your son (daughter) and he (she) will give you peace; he will bring delight to your soul" (Prov. 29:17, NIV).

I am aware of the need to construct a positive relationship with the students. It is important to do this during the first fifteen minutes each morning. This is done through the use of affirmations (see Appendix V) and teaches them structure.

This sets the tone for the rest of the day. It is beneficial academically, socially, and it builds character.

My next book, *A Teacher's Guide to a Peaceful Classroom,* has a variety of these strategies that will assist our children in gaining confidence and making them team players.

When schools and homes are using the same tools for the advancement of our children, it solidifies both efforts. We should not be going in opposite directions and wondering why it's so difficult to solve the problems.

Rules and laws govern our classes and homes. It's okay to say, "We all must follow the rules or laws of this house in order to maintain a peaceful home." Teamwork makes the dream work.

In Myles Munroe's Daily Devotional Potential for Every Day, p. 349, he refers to Proverbs 13:13 "he who scorns instruction will pay for it, but he who respects a command is rewarded." He writes, "The child who lives with no rules and restrictions is much more likely to get hurt or end up in trouble than the child who lives within a structure of parental guidance."

Therefore parents, stand them up, build them up on the inside and no one can tear them down on the outside. No one can take away what's on the inside of them.

You are guided by your own words. So what do you say about you? Say what God says about you. "Whoever gives heed to instruction prospers and blessed is he who trusts in the Lord (Prov. 16:2, NIV).

"Listen my son to your father's instruction and do not forsake your mother's teaching" (Prov. 1:8-9, NIV). Wise parents know children's hearts, skills, and gifts will guide them through God's teachings. You will have all of them on your lips. "A wise man's heart guides his mouth, and his lips promote instruction". Pleasant words are a honeycomb sweet to the soul and healing to the bones" (Prov. 16:23-24, NIV).

Continuous unpleasant words are sour to the soul and will not promote healing. Constant barrages of negative words will tear down all family members—and all manner of illness will arise. It is crucial that we learn how to build each other up and not tear each other down.

Parents, educators, pastors, and all who work with our children must help our children "to fan into flame the gift of God, which is in you (them) for God did not give us a spirit of (fear) timidity, but a spirit of power of love and of self-discipline (sound mind)" (1 Tim. 1:6-7, NIV).

Since God did not give us a spirit of fear and timidity, why do we have it? He didn't give us hate or tell us not to be disciplined. God gave us what we need for living a successful life.

Let's do it! He gave us the power to be!

Her Story: All About Me

I graduated from Southern Illinois University in Carbondale, Illinois with a BS degree in Elementary Education and a minor in Spanish. I taught in the Carbondale school system for two years. My husband and I relocated to Springfield, IL where I was employed in the Springfield Public School System.

In 1978, we moved to Cedar Rapids, Iowa. I taught at Taylor Elementary school. At Taylor Elementary, I developed and initiated my program, Towards Affective Development (TAD). Toward Affective Development (TAD) is youth effecting change from within.

I noted that a large number of my students were continually putting each other down. This behavior was affecting the classroom climate. The students' attention to the Put-Downs made it difficult to teach and, of course, this negative behavior was affecting their grades.

I recognized that these students needed something else that would allow them to see the number of Put-Downs that occurred during the day.

Thanks to the counselor who jumped right in to assist and provide support for the program, TAD was born. I presented my new program to the principal. He was enthusiastic and was looking forward to seeing its outcome.

The counselor recorded a baseline count of the daily number of Put-Downs for one month, which would later be compared with their behavior after the introduction of TAD.

It was obvious that they needed an inside change. Thus, my program, Towards Affective Development, was created. TAD means youth affecting change within. I know you have seen these words before.

The term "Tadpoles" was recently added to the program here in Richmond, Virginia. My friend, Loretta Woodson, saw the letters T̲, A̲, and D̲, and thought of tadpoles and how they are transformed into frogs. Her thought was that the tadpoles would grow into responsible adults.

I counted the number of Put-Downs with a golf counter for the first base count and subsequent counts for the remainder of the year. The students were curious about the constant clicking sounds all day long. I told them I would let them know later.

After a month, I had a class meeting to let them know what I was doing. I had made a chart and graphed the daily Put-Downs. I showed them the Put-Down Chart. During the first few days, there were fifty to a hundred Put-Downs. We discussed this at our first class meeting. They were very surprised by the high numbers. We discussed the reasons the thoughtless comments and how each had felt when being put-down. Each time I heard a put-down, I clicked. Soon they began to think before putting someone down. I didn't fuss. I just clicked. I also let them know I would continue graphing the Put-Downs.

By the next meeting on the next Friday, they had cut the Put-Downs to twenty-five. It was hilarious to see them put a finger over their mouths when they were about to say a Put-Down. They became motivated to refrain from making thoughtless statements about other students.

We met each Friday and compared weekly charts, noting progress. Their mission was to have the best classroom in the school. They were happy, and I could teach without having to stop to correct negative behavior.

By the end of the year, we had a **Positive Remark Chart** where the golf counter was also used to count positive remarks. We continued comparing charts. They actually went off the chart with more than a hundred positive remarks in one day. Everyone was happy and smiling; of course, their grades improved.

The most wonderful thing was when a new student arrived in our room with a huge chip on his shoulder. He constantly caused conflict in the classroom. I watched as the third graders took over. I did not have to say anything to him. They would not sit beside him. They moved their desks far away from him and would not talk to, or play with him.

After a few days he recognized what was going on. For most of the day, he put his head on the desk. This all happened the first week he was there.

One day someone said, "You are not going to come in Mrs. Braxton's class and act like that! We don't have Put-Downs in here! We all get along!"

Guess what? His behavior changed immediately.

At our next Class Meeting (see Appendix for a sample), we discussed what had occurred. Their grades were awesome. What a year! TAD has continued for me ever since—at every school with variations.

Out of TAD came the peaceful classroom, the peaceful home, and my next book: *A Teacher's Guide to a Peaceful Classroom*.

The essential part that came from a positive, peaceful classroom was seeing students begin to change from within at school and at home.

I feel blessed to have been given this book so that many families can watch their children change from within to become more responsible, to recognize their boundaries, and to fulfill their destinies.

I dearly love my profession. God has put me on a mission to penetrate homes in a positive manner in order to assist in areas where they lack knowledge, understanding, and the skills necessary to know how to bring about peace that will remain in their homes. I have come to realize that if parents knew better, they would do better.

I have a passion for children who have been hurt. I have a passion for children who need to find out who they are and how to get the most out of life, fulfilling their potential.

When we are hurt, we act in certain negative ways. We retreat, agree with the perpetrators, and turn on ourselves by acting out in inappropriate ways. We hurt—so we hurt others. We don't even try to get better on our own. We feel worthless. We wonder why we should try. A few helping hands, compassion, and lots of prayer is what we need.

We seldom think! *Neither that thing nor person that hurt me so much will stop me. I'm going to do the opposite of what was done to me!*

I don't like to tell this story because, even at this age, it still hurts. To undergo the experience of presenting my story, I have to look up to keep tears from welling up.

In the eighth grade, we were reading *Florence Nightingale*. Our class sat in rows and each of us had to read. I was in the very last seat in the back of the room. When it was my turn to read, I couldn't pronounce a word.

The teacher said, "You're stupid! You will never make anything of yourself!"

I wanted to die! I wanted the floor to open and swallow me! What she said couldn't have taken a split second, but it seemed like hours.

As the class continued reading, I could hardly hear or see because of the tears. Somebody in the class started to read and couldn't pronounce the same word; however, the teacher told her the word, making no condescending or negative remarks to or about the other reader.

That's when I made up my mind to do something, be somebody—even in the midst of the pain and hurt. I decided, right then and there, what I was going to be. I was going to be a teacher—and I was going to be the best teacher a child would ever have.

I knew I could go to my physical education teacher with my hurt and tears. She embraced me. She had believed in me, for she had previously made me the captain of the cheerleading squad. Her words to me were, "Don't let that stop you!" "You can be whatever you want to be!" When I went to college, it was all about showing her that I could be somebody! After a while, it was not about her. It became my mission to teach—and then it became a passion. I was driven to exceed at each school in which I taught. Following is a list of accomplishments that came my way as I strived to be the best teacher I could be: Master Teacher in Springfield, Illinois; The birth of TAD/Towards Affective Development; Youth affecting change from within, Cedar Rapids, Iowa; Richmond, VA, Teacher of the Year, 2 consecutive years at Reid Elementary School; nominated for the REB Awards for Teachers of Excellence; Who's Who of Elementary Teachers 1995; Facilitator for Community of Caring; National Trainer of Teachers for the Joseph P. Kennedy Foundations Community of Caring-Founder, Eunice Kennedy Shriver; Selected to serve on a national committee to develop an elementary school curriculum guide for ethics; National Trainer of Trainers for the Community of Caring Trainer's Manual.

I hesitated to write this section. In fact, I decided to write it just before I submitted my final edit of the book. My reason for hesitancy was that I feared others would think I was bragging. Then I thought that I had mentioned some of the accomplishments in other chapters. I wanted to use it as a catalyst for others who have been hurt and are stuck in the same old rut. You can do it. Again, I say, "Go confidently in the direction of your dream."(Thoreau) You have heard these words number of times, haven't you?

That's where I am at this point—and it is the reason I couldn't stay retired. I will teach forever. There will never be another retirement. No matter how busy I get, I want to keep a pulse on this profession.

Adults must look closely at the defining events that have caused us to be where we are at this point. That event could have had a negative or positive effect on my life. It is our choice as adults to move on in spite of what has happened. We can use it as a catalyst to catapult us to new heights.

Some of you may be wondering why I was so transparent about my insecurities, as I mentioned them so often. I found it necessary to be transparent so that it left no doubt in your mind that nothing is impossible when you refuse to give up. Whatever you dream you are capable to of doing can become your reality. *Goethe's Couplet* reinforces this belief. Recall what Henry David Thoreau said, "Go confidently in the direction of your dream."

Whenever you know beyond a shadow of a doubt that God inspired you to do a certain thing, know this, He will keep prompting you until you get it done. It may take you years to do it, but you will get it done **IF** you believe in yourself. It takes faith to hang in there. When all the adversities keep coming relentlessly, then things begin to fall into place unexpectedly. Blessings will begin overtaking you at every turn, and all these blessings will come upon you and overtake you if you listen to the voice of your God (Deut. 28:2, NIV).

Every person I told about my book said, "I can't wait, let me know," or "I will buy one and even buy some as a gift for friends," or "Let me know when you have your books signing. I will be there." One person said, "I will buy a box of books from you. I will give them to people." No one asked about the price. I didn't even know the cost, or how many books would be in a box. One person offered her home for my first book signing

I was invited to school PTA meetings and churches to discuss it and to sign books. My church, Faith Landmarks Ministry was one of the churches.

This has not been an easy task. I had no idea about the intricacies of writing for publication. It has taken me nearly three years to complete it. I didn't give up. There were times when I thought I would give out. The number of hours per day and night was taxing.

I didn't say I didn't think about giving up. I thought about it many times. But God kept reminding me that this book was not for me, it was to assist parents and their children to choose a new and different avenue on which to travel. I couldn't quit because I know that my experience and successes in classrooms in four cities could be duplicated in family homes with little experience and/or expense.

All that is needed are willing children and adults who want peace at home. It can be done through the establishment of *Home Meetings*, which is the key. If your home is in turmoil, with discord among family members, children failing in school, and family relationships are dysfunctional, this book is for you. Learning to conduct home meetings, with all family members functioning as active participants, you can create and maintain your peaceful home. Without a peaceful home, the house and family unit will continue to crumble into more dysfunctional pieces.

As I was entering the last stage of writing and editing and preparing for the marketing stage, *EVERYTHING* went wrong! I don't have time and space to enumerate the events that created a picture that looked like a disaster happening before my eyes.

Trafford, my publishing company had completed stage three. It was time for me to complete the intricate task of editing and returning the book to them for final publication. Due to my lack of typing skills, I knew it would take me a while (a long while) to get the job done. I began to pray.

I began to feel anxious, but I prayed, knowing that I had to get beyond what was going on in my mind. I found scriptures to help me lean on God to see me through this step. I was almost there.

Let me remind you or tell you that God has already worked it out! If we would just believe that, let go and let God keep His promise that

He made for us before we were conceived in our mother's womb(Jer. 5:1, NIV), we would see, and we would have what He said we would have.

For the last time I will refer to Goethe's Couplet.

> *. . . The moment one definitely commits oneself,*
> *Providence moves in.*
> *God is Providence.*
> *All sorts of things occur which would never have occurred.*
> *A whole stream of events issues from that decision,*
> *Raising in one's favor all manner of unforeseen incidents*
> *And meetings and material assistance,*
> *Who no man could have dreamt would come his way.*

God is awesome! He had made a way that I could never have dreamed would come my way. My college friend, Janet, who is now a world evangelist is literally following God's command to "***Go into the entire world and preach the Gospel . . .***"(Matt. 29:19, NIV), and is doing just that.

I had neither seen nor talked to Janet in about seven years. She called me hoping I had the same phone number, and left a message telling me she would be in Williamsburg, Virginia, conducting a 3-day women's conference and asking if I would come to her conference.

Of course I went to see and hear my friend speak about the countries she had visited and the success of her ministry of winning souls for Christ. She had visited Jerusalem and the surrounding area 68 times! I was inspired and impressed with how God had blessed her.

At the conclusion of the conference a few participants were sitting and talking, and I mentioned that I had written a book and was completing the last stage of editing and would then be ready for the marketing stage. There was a lady sitting with us, Lynda, who said, "Oh, I edit books for people." "I love editing. I commented, 'Oh, that's wonderful!" We shared telephone numbers, but I didn't give it any more thought. This was yet another encounter that I had not recognized as God 'ordering my steps' to completing my goal.

Later, during my agitated editing stage, considering the time it would take me to do the editing alone, I was awakened early one morning and thought about Lynda, and actually saw her face. A voice said, "Call Lynda."

I immediately called her, identified myself as Pat Braxton, and she replied, "Oh, hi Pat. I was just thinking of you yesterday, and wondering how you were coming along with the book." With surprise I told her about my early morning experience of seeing her face and that God had told me to call her. I asked her to help me with the editing. She agreed to help, and expressed gratitude in being one of the first to read my book. Lynda and I met four times to discuss what needed to be cut from and/or added to the content. She also worked at home. I told her I would have to put her on my payroll as I expected her to assist me with the next book; *A Teacher's Guide to a Peaceful Classroom.* She readily agreed to help me edit.

Lynda is a retired, 40 year veteran educator who loves children. She has taught exceptional children, facilitated reading instructional programs, and retired as an elementary school administrator. She is currently a part-time instructor of military spouses and family members in a regional General Educational Development (GED) class, serving a high population of students who speak English as a second language.

I said all of this to emphasize that God will move heaven and earth to keep His promises to us if we have faith in Him. I will recap what He showed me about this encounter . . . *Pat needs help editing. I knew she would need this help before she was born. Although she has not seen or heard from her friend Janet for a while, I will bring her from across the world. I will interrupt her many travels, saving souls and bring her to Virginia so that Pat can meet Lynda who is willing to help her edit her book. She will be glad, even overjoyed to do it . . .* That's how God works. We can trust Him to keep His word.

Thank you, Lynda, for you truly are a God send to me. Thank you, Janet, for obeying the call to come to Williamsburg in order to enlighten us to reach for God's promises and to bless others.

Potential: What about You?

"There's a wealth of potential in you. You must decide if you're going to rob the world or bless it with the rich, valuable, potent untapped resources locked inside you."
—Myles Munroe

These words struck a deep cord within me. I wondered how many adults have robbed the world of untapped resources—and how many of our children will do the same.

I neglected to reach my potential. Many people expected me to make presentations at conferences and PTAs. They wanted me to search deeper inside and share the gifts of teaching with a wider audience than the classrooms of elementary school children. It seemed obvious to them that my next step should be doing something I love, sharing my beliefs with others. Years and years passed before I took the big step.

God stepped in and reminded me that I had not yet met my potential. I was awakened in the middle of the morning with the title of this book. I told people I was going to write a book about education.

God reminded me of my duty to fulfill my potential, which came out of my profession. My mission turned into my passion. That's when that passion turned to hunger that was pushing me even when I was tired.

It is my desire that this guide will cause you to look at your potential as we guide your children together to reach their potential. Give them a chance to see a renewed energy to guide yourself and the family to reach their potential. They should have seen their "new" mom or dad surface during many incidents. Their respect for you will be heightened as you direct the family meetings.

Integrity, compassion, responsibility, and discipline will rule your home. The family place is at peace. The siblings are doing their chores and reaping the benefits of completing their jobs. The Character Chart has built character in each individual and they have been validated.

The use of the "Fuss Buster" Calendar has caused each of them to receive some things they actually worked for and even **earned** money. You didn't forget the home Award Ceremonies for earning better grades, for doing all homework, and improving behavior at home and school.

They are enjoying Positive Bombardment when each sibling stands in the center of the circle while everyone bombards them with Positive Remarks.

Remember to use the "95 Ways to Praise Your Children." The Think Sheet caused them to think and write about the rules they broke and played a giant role in building character. The Friday Awards Ceremony, videos, food and fun night caused the family to grow and appreciate each other more.

Not only is your home peaceful, but the school, students, and teachers are ecstatic about the wonderful things that have happened around your house. Your children see you as a role model. No longer will they look outside the home for someone to mimic. You are training and teaching them how to become the first and best teacher for their family when they grow up. You are passing on the legacy.

By this time, you should be ready to think about yourself. Over a period of time, you have been doing what was necessary to bring about a peaceful home.

Do you have a dream? Have you ever had a dream? Now is the right time. Thinking about yourself and your potential does not mean you will forget about your family. On the contrary, your family will be glad to see your devote time to your dreams. They are more confident in themselves and each other and are headed toward their potential. You provided that!

Go ahead. Go to that closet and find those old desires and dreams. Dust off the cobwebs. Dare to dream. Before going to bed tonight, really think about your big dream.

Don't forget to go before God and tell Him, (as if he doesn't already know!). He just wanted you to know and tell Him. "Before I formed you in the womb, I knew you: before you were born I set you apart. I appointed you as a prophet to the nations" (Jer. 1:5, NIV). Think about that. "For I know the plans I have for you declares the Lord, plans to prosper you and not to harm you, plans to give you a hope and a future (Jer. 29:11, NIV). The Lord said he will give you a hope and a future.

You will see there are no reasons for excuses. You can't claim you're not good enough, you had family problems, you had too many failed relationships, your boyfriend, husband, sister, mother died, you were molested, or you have no money. You don't need money for an idea or a dream. If you let God lead you, He will make a way for you to complete that dream. You need faith and perseverance.

Many people have realized their potential. What about you? There's a wealth of potential in you. You must decide if you're going to rob the world or fill it with the rich, valuable, potent, untapped resources locked inside you. (Myles Munroe)

You have read my story. You can't use age as a reason for not moving ahead. You are reading my first book. There are four more books that are coming and scripture stickers that are being revised. If you are still alive, God wants you to have faith in His word and prove Him true by showing the world around you His providence.

I am not boasting of myself. I am boasting of a God who keeps His word if we will keep our word. We must **Be** the people (in our hearts) God wants us to be: **Do** whatever it takes, using biblical principles to avoid hurting others: and we will then **Have** all He has planned for us—and we will be able to bless many people.

All excuses have been taken away. Think about the impact you will make on your children as they see you sitting with them studying, working on your dream, and completing it!

> Write down the revelation and make it plain on tablets so that a herald may run with it. For the revelation awaits an appointed time; it speaks of the end and will not prove false. Though it lingers wait for it; it will certainly come and not delay. (Hab. 2:2-3, NIV)

Since God had to make a plan to create the world and all that is in it, why would we think we don't have to make plans? Writing them down helps us see our progress. I recommend you date and time your work. It's exciting to look back and see where we came from, where we are now, and where we are going.

There will be times—some hard, some flourishing. Keep your eyes on God and keep repeating His Word until it becomes a part of you.

See it in your mind's eye. See it unfold in full color. Write down what you see and date it. It is important to remember that the plan for you and your dream has already been formed in your mother's womb. Don't give up. It certainly will come without delay.

The Wrap-Up

Thank You, Father, For:

- entrusting me to write this book
- for the many souls saved
- for the many families that have become united
- for national teams working to save our kids
- for the world community
- for the students who will fulfill their destiny, completing their education by becoming city, state, national, and world leaders
- for parents who will leave an inheritance to their children's children
- for the children's children who will leave a legacy
- for their children for less crime and murder
- for less incarceration
- for fewer people dealing drugs
- for fewer dropouts
- for fewer unwanted pregnancies

I have deliberately tried to touch your heart to show that we have come together to bridge the gap to bring about a caring nation under the banner of our children. I want all of us to know it is our responsibility. Our children are worth whatever we can all do together. They are our future. What this present generation looks like is what we permitted it to look like.

You have learned how to prepare them at home before sending them to school. They are ready! Intervention techniques were used to prevent further disasters to overcome our offspring and prevent further damage to God's precious creation. You have been guided in how to build character values in your children through Family Meetings. Most importantly, you have learned that you are the first teacher. You must go first so they can see that you have transformed yourself into a beautiful butterfly. They need not look outside their home because the treasures are in their house. You are their "hero" or "shero" outside of God. Now there is unity in the house.

You became different because you did things differently. Now you have a peaceful home!

There is absolutely no reason not to start now. "Now" written backward spells "won." You have won!

Through this guidebook, I present you with a happy, healthy haven. Now together we have all won. Enough said. Let's get started.

Love to you,

Patricia Ann Powell-Braxton

The Plan of Salvation

Each time I sat down to write, I had to ask God for his help for each section. I had to pray in the name of Jesus, knowing that my prayers would be answered.

Inspiration came at different times during the day or night. The fear I had of writing at the beginning was lifted as I knew I was being instructed what to write.

After a while, I couldn't wait to start writing again. At times, hilarious thoughts were streaming in—and I was laughing as I wrote. At other times my eyes would be filled with tears.

This guide was written for the children and parents. Whatever you need, God is there. I would love to lead you to this God through his Son Jesus Christ, if you don't already know Him.

"Jesus said, I am the gate, whoever enters through me will be saved" (Jn. 10:9). "And everyone who calls on the name of Jesus will be saved" (Acts 2:21, NIV).

> The word is near you; it is in your mouth and in your heart, that is the word of faith we are proclaiming; that if you confess with your mouth that Jesus is Lord and believe in your heart that God raised him from the dead you will be saved. For it is with your heart that you believe and are justified, and it is with your mouth that you confess and are saved. (Rom. 10:8-10, NIV)

If you confess your sins with your mouth, then you are saved. Now go tell others. You have done the most important thing that you can do.

As you walk in this new life, transformation will be apparent to your children and all who know you for you will be looking like Jesus. I included this plan because it is the most crucial element you can leave with your family that will last for eternity.

Be Ready!

I was substituting for a kindergarten class in May 2012. All five of the kindergarten classes had gone to the cafeteria to practice for the June graduation. We had lined them up on stage and on the floor. Alice Lilly walked to the edge of the stage to change the CD when she caught her foot on the stage lights. She stumbled and fell to the floor, face down at my feet. As she was falling, she looked me in the eye.

When I looked down, blood was flowing. I immediately got down on my knees and began to pray while touching her back. The school nurse was trying to keep her awake by asking her questions.

The paramedics arrived and said, "We will have to take her to MCV Trauma Unit." MCV Hospital is about thirty-five minutes away. I could understand why they were taking her there because of the apparent extensive damage to her head, face and shoulder.

When they put her on the gurney, she awakened and screamed! I was standing behind the paramedics. I asked where they were going to take her. They apparently had a change of mind and said they would take her to Chippenham Hospital, which was about five minutes away.

Alice had broken three bones in her left shoulder, and there was significant damage to her forehead. The doctor said, "She was lucky to be alive." He named five concerns that could have been fatal during the fall.

I said, "Alice is **blessed** to be alive, considering the height from which she fell, face-down."

In talking with her, I was surprised that she could even speak clearly enough for me to hear and understand her if I listened closely! O course, she was on mass doses of medicine. Alice told me an amazing story! She related in great detail that she had an out-of-body experience as she lay on that hard tile floor!

Alice remembered that she had been detached from the body lying on the floor. She said, "I was going up in an extremely bright light!" She recalled, "I was very excited as I was traveling toward the light!" She stopped when she heard some words. She said, "What are those words—and why are they being said? That is Pat praying in the Spirit!"

Alice said she hesitated, thinking about how pleasant she felt and wondered if she should turn and go back. She felt the urge to go back.

She turned around and came back. When she told me that, I was in tears. Her daughter, Allison, said, "Now, that is the kind of friend to have."

The doctor previously said that he probably would have to operate on her shoulder. It wasn't long after the accident and physical therapy that the doctor decided that the operation would not be necessary—and she is healing quite well

When the Spirit tells us to do a thing, we listen and obey. I tell you this story to inform you that nothing is too hard for God (Gen. 18:14, NIV), therefore, nothing is too hard for you (Jer. 32:17, NIV). We are to be in season whenever it is necessary. "I give you charge: Preach the word. Be prepared in season and out of season." (2 Tim. 4:2, NIV)

God's Hand Again!

Just as I was preparing again to send my manuscript to Trafford, God opened up yet another opportunity for me to use TAD/Towards Affective Development's strategies introduced in this guide as the Master Teacher.

Victory Academy, a school located at the Family Worship Center in Richmond, Virginia, will reopen in the fall of 2013 for kindergartners to grade 3. Enrollment will be low, with forty-five students, a ratio of one to eleven or twelve students. This ratio will serve as a critical piece in assisting the school to reach its' mission by helping every child succeed.

This will impact the home through building strong relations between the school, parents, and the child. You will recognize this as the Equilateral Triangle in Appendix VIII.

Again, you will recognize this new opportunity in Goethe's Couplet as one of those "unforeseen incidences and meetings" which came through my mentor, Sheary Johnson ED. D.

Appendix I

Towards Affective Development Program At-Home Tips

1. Behavior Change (+) (-)
   A. Impacts grades (+) (-)
      1. (+) Behavior = Rewards
      2. (-) Behavior = Family Meeting
         a. Set Rules
2. Refuse to buy them ANYTHING until behavior is (+) and they are on Green!
3. Calendar (see Appendix)
   On the back of calendar, have children make a list of things they would like to do or have. Set dates when they may be able to do these things. Of course, it's dependent on whether they have fulfilled their responsibilities at school and home.
4. Refuse to buy them anything new until there is a (+) behavior change at home and school.

Appendix II

Towards Affective Development Contract

Child

I _____ promise to be the best I can be by listening and following directions each day at home, school, church, and in the neighborhood.

I promise to follow the Chore Chart and the Character Chart to the best of my ability. This includes home chores and homework for school.

If I break the contract, I know what the consequences will be, and I will adhere to them without showing anger.

Parent

As the parent/guardian/caregiver, I promise to fulfill my role as the adult; to use the meeting for roles, rules and duties. The rules and duties will be made clear at that time. Any breaking of the rules will result in known consequences.

If we all do our part, we will have the best **Peaceful Home** there can be. Place your signature all over this page if you agree.

Appendix III

You Are a Marvel
(Pablo Casals)

Each second we live is a new and unique moment
Of the universe, a moment that will never be again
. . . And what do we teach our children? We teach
Them two and two make four, and that Paris is
The capital of France.
When will we also teach them what they are?
We should say to each of them: Do you know
What you are? You are a marvel. You are unique. In
All the years that have passed, there has never been
Another child like you. Your legs, your arms, your
Clever fingers, the way you move
You may become a Shakespeare, a Michelangelo,
A Beethoven. You have the capacity for anything, Yes,
You are a marvel. And when you grow up, can you
Then harm another who is like you, a marvel?
You must work—we must all work—to make the
World worthy of its children.

Appendix IV

95 Ways to Praise a Child

Wow * Way to Go * Super * You're Special * Outstanding * Excellent * Great * Good * Neat * Well Done * Remarkable * I Knew You Could Do It * I'm Proud of You * Fantastic * Super Star * Nice Work * Looking Good * You're on Top of It * Beautiful * Now You're Flying * You're Catching On * Bravo * Now You've Got It * You're Incredible * How Nice * You're Fantastic * Hurray for You * How Smart * You're on Target * You're on Your Way * Good Job * That's Incredible * Hot Dog * Dynamite * Bingo * You're Unique * Nothing Can Stop You Now * Good for You * You're a Winner * Remarkable Job * Beautiful Work * Spectacular * You're Spectacular * You're Precious * Great Discovery * Fantastic Job * You've Discovered the Secret * You Figured It Out * Hip, Hip Hurray * Magnificent * Marvelous * Terrific * You're Important * Phenomenal * You're Sensational * Super Work * Creative Job * Super Job * Fantastic Job * Exceptional Performance * You Are a Real Trooper * You Are Responsible * You Are Exciting * You Care * You Learned It Right * What an Imagination * What a Good Listener * You Are Fun * You Belong * You're Growing Up * You Tried Hard * You're A-Okay, Buddy * Beautiful Sharing * Outstanding Performance * You're a Good Friend * I Trust You * You're Important * You Mean a Lot to Me * You Make Me Happy * You Make Me Laugh * You've Got a Friend * You're a Joy * I Respect You * You Brighten My Day * Awesome * You Mean the World to Me * You Made My Day * That's Correct * You're a Treasure * That's the Best * You're Wonderful * You're Perfect * A+ Job * P.S. Remember, a Smile Is Worth 100 Words!

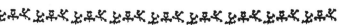

Appendix V

Affirmations

Ask each child to learn from memory the poems and sayings you have posted around your home. Regularly, make it a practice to make these words a part of their conversation. Soon they will become a part of them. These words will form their behavior and change negative behavior into positive behavior.

You as parents and guardians are shaping their destiny. The potential for greatness is inside of your child/children. It just needs to be nurtured through love. Take the time to build this in and for their future.

Because I Am Somebody!

I am somebody.
I need somebody.
Somebody needs me.
Everybody needs somebody.
Everybody is somebody to somebody.
Nobody, but nobody, can make me feel like a nobody,
Because I Am Somebody!

Today

Today is the first day of the rest of my life.
I will make the best of it
I will do my best in following directions and listening.
If I do these things, I will be the best person I could be.
—Patricia Braxton

Act the way you want to be and soon you'll be the way you act.
—Anonymous

Your attitude determines your altitude.
—Anonymous

Appendix VI

Words to Remember

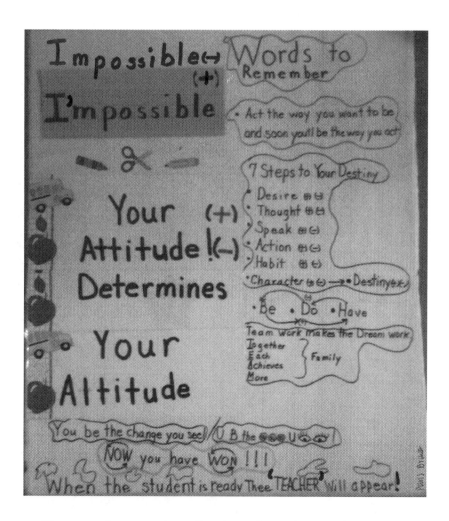

This poster hangs on the wall and is to be used at Family Meetings.

Appendix VII

The Umbrella Principle

The upright umbrella is used at schools and in Family Meetings to depict the student who is not listening or following directions, and indicates the likely negative results on their grades.

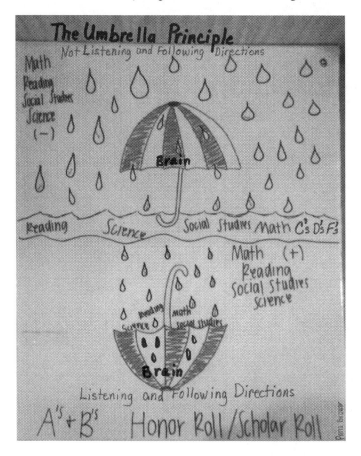

The inverted umbrella depicts the student who listens and follows directions and who is more likely to master the subjects.

Appendix VIII

A Visual Look at Communication through Equilateral Triangles

Triangle 1 shows a balanced flow of communication without broken lines. The parent, teacher, and student are in constant contact.

Triangle 2 shows some communication, but the lines of communication are broken between the student, teacher, and/or parent.

Triangle 3 shows many broken lines of communication between the student, parent, and teacher.

In Triangles 2 and 3 it is not difficult to see who loses—the student!

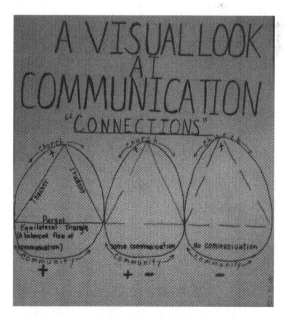

Appendix IX

Fuss Buster Calendar

Sun	Mon	Tue	Wed	Thu	Fri	Sat

Note: Children's names and their lists of sites and activities chosen as rewards for positive behavior should appear on the back of the calendar.

Appendix X

Think Sheet

Student Name _____

Teacher _____ Date _____

This is the rule I broke: _____

_____

_____

I chose to break this rule because: _____

_____

_____

_____

_____

Who was bothered when I broke this rule? _____

_____

_____

This is what I could have done instead: _____

_____

_____

_____

Student Signature _____ Date _____
Parent Signature _____ Date _____
Teacher Signature _____ Date _____
Principal Signature _____ Date _____

Appendix XI

Character Chart

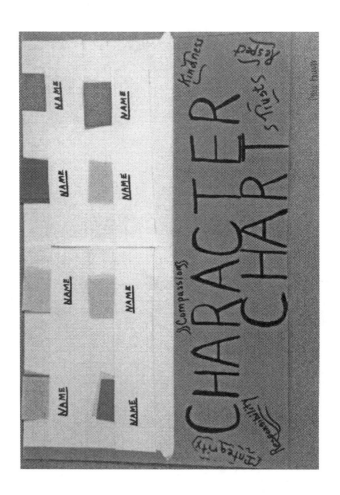

Appendix XII

Job Chart

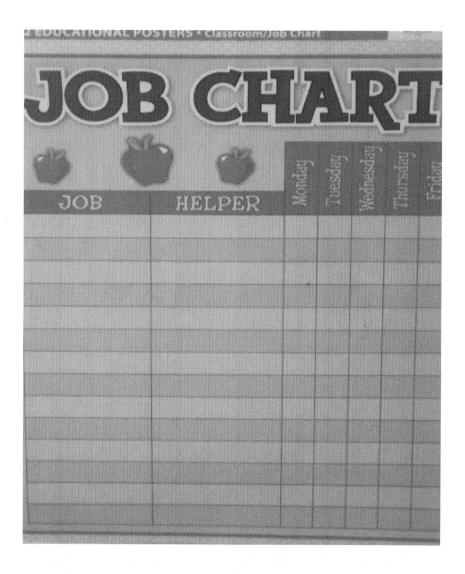

Appendix XIII

Foundations Chart

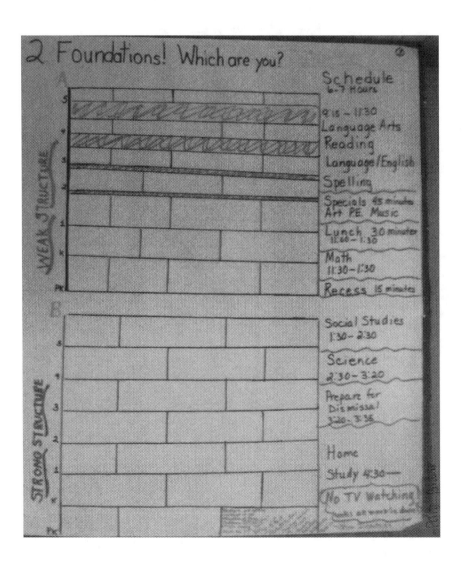

Appendix XIV

Goethe's Couplet

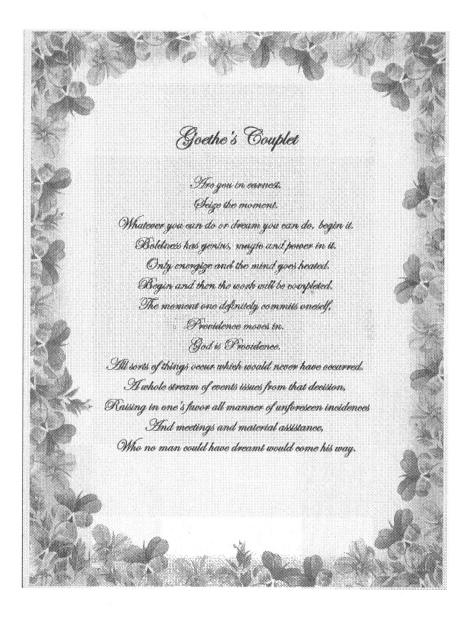

Goethe's Couplet

Are you in earnest,

Seize the moment.

Whatever you can do or dream you can do, begin it.

Boldness has genius, magic and power in it.

Only energize and the mind goes heated.

Begin and then the work will be completed.

The moment one definitely commits oneself,

Providence moves in.

God is Providence.

All sorts of things occur which would never have occurred,

A whole stream of events issues from that decision,

Raising in one's favor all manner of unforeseen incidences

And meetings and material assistance,

Who no man could have dreamt would come his way.

Appendix XV

Class Meeting Minutes

(Example of minutes recorded by a student)

May 10, 2001   Class Meeting

What went well today.

1. People were acting nice to each other.
2. Saying please & I forgive you
3. Showing respect for others
4. It wasn't many fights
5. More people showing integrity
6. People were acting like family
7. Less people getting in trouble behaving
8. People let other people borrow things and giving back Responsibility
9. Trust & integrity
10. More people help each other
11. People show friendship
12. Being Trustworthy

Reid Elementary School
Grade 5
Richmond, Virginia

Resources

Introduction

Parents and caregivers, as I neared the end of this guide, I felt it necessary to provide you with a few resources to assist you on your new journey with your children. You may already be aware of these resources. I believe you will take the initiative to find resources for your individual interests.

Our national and local radio station's personalities, like Sheilah Belle, "Community" Clovia Lawrence and Reggie B., as well as other community agencies and military troops, have committed themselves to community services like, back to school supply programs; coat, shoe, mitten, glove, clothes drives; Christmas Angels; Toys for Tots; angel trees and much more.

Churches have their own drives which add to the services that our radio stations commit themselves to, such as mentors who assist our children in learning to read, write, do math, practice appropriate social behavior skills and more. Providing some students with Lunch Buddies on a yearly basis is a huge builder of character that boosts their self-esteem. As I have stated, I am privileged to see that "special" facial expression as they interact with their Buddy while having lunch. Please volunteer for this program. You may never know the value you brought to them, but they will never forget it. I remember when these services occurred mostly on certain holidays. The saying, "It takes a village (community) to raise a child," has expanded on an even larger scale. It's been raised to another level.

The word *community* is growing in many organizations. CNN's Education Nation, which occurs in September, permits us to have a look into issues that face our schools in our cities and states. Many issues affect our communities and impact our states in an adverse way. Parents, teachers and students come together in a summit to discuss the problems with resolution in mind. If you miss the airing of this program, go to www.educationnation.com. Program producers look for volunteers with ideas, and who will assist in this noble effort.

Our national television and radio stations' personalities, both male and female, have taken on larger causes that are personal to them. They all have this in common; mentoring, education/scholarships; career path; prison initiatives; and retreats for young people to spend time with the personalities in order for them to see that people care. I mentioned earlier that children don't care how much you know until they know how much you care. The celebrities are showing whose responsibility it is by their involvement. These personalities are impacting this generation's youth in order to change their vision of the world from one of negativity to a positive one.

Many students have received computers, I Pads, scholarships and much more. Adults have received mentoring and advice on health and lifestyle; also, how to live a Godly life. There are people who do not have a church home and have received Christ through the media.

These personalities make themselves visible as they bring unity in the community through their visits to the cities throughout the United States. There is a call on their lives and it is through their diligence that they press on.

I had the distinct pleasure of interviewing Mr. Bowling, Director of Marketing in Corporate Relations of Big Brothers and Big Sisters Organization (BBBS) in Richmond, VA. Mr. Bowling related that he was featured on the Michael Baisden Radio One Show for the innovative ways he used to recruit volunteers for Big Brothers and Big Sister Clubs. He has worked with a student, Tyquan, for two years. I asked if he had seen any progress in the student during the two year period. His response was that Tyquan had begun to open up and had become more motivated at school. His grades had also improved. In a letter Tyquan wrote to Mr. Bowling, he told him that he had always been there for him and had never disappointed him. That speaks volumes for the mentoring/tutorial relationship Mr. Bowling had forged with Tyquan. As he was recalling the heartfelt words from this 4th grade boy, Mr. Bowling's voice cracked.

The good news is that the black fraternities and sororities form Virginia Commonwealth, Virginia Union, and Virginia State universities are volunteering to mentor some boys and girls. "These are just a few volunteers that are listed in the Richmond, Virginia area and there are 250 boys that are listed that need volunteers," stated Mr. Bowling. He said that these are the ones on record. "We know there are thousands not listed."

What is preventing us from finding volunteer help for our boys and girls who lack parental support in their homes? We can't blame others for what we could or should be doing ourselves. Let us use this wonderful resource, BBBS, and volunteer in each of these United States of America because we are our Brother's (Sister's) keepers. (Website—bbbs.org, and Nations website—(zip code for area) big.bro. bigsis.com)

Another local and national resource that has assisted millions of boys and girls over on hundred years is the Boy's and Girl's Clubs of America. In 2012, this organization celebrated one hundred years of service. You do the math. There have to be millions of boys and girls who, as Denzel Washington, President, and Jennifer Lopez, spokesperson, say, ". . . follow a path." "For many, that path will lead to a door, a door that gives them a place to grow, learn, to belong; a place to forge the future." "These doors transform them as they did for us," says Mr. Washington.

I gained a new respect for the Boy's and Girl's Club as I listen to the end of the school day announcement about the transportation van that takes some boys and girls to the club. Not only do they afford the children a place to keep them off the streets, safe and alive, they also are mentored, assisted with their academics (homework), are well fed with character building and sports activities and much more.

Again, I ask for volunteers to assist. I don't believe they can ever have too much help. (www.infocbgca.org; Denzel Washington President of Boy's and Girl's Clubs of America; boys and girls club facil: mentor to the masses)

Susan Burton is another of those "unforeseen incidences and meetings . . . that no man could have dreamt would have come his way," mentioned in Goethe's Couplet. My friend, LuVada, introduced her to me one Sunday morning after church. LuVada knew we both had something in common; love for children and how to advance them. We met, talked and exchanged phone numbers. She was interested in my book's potential to encourage parents and students to grow and work together in unity. I had just met another lady who had a heart for children and communities. Susan is a board member for PMI Project, Project Management Institute, which had made its first venture in the nation in Henrico Public School System, Henrico County, Virginia.

Jennifer Romeo-Green is President of PM Project Harmony, a non-profit organization. It is a unique, as well as, the first project management program, called *"Flipm"*. The kid's parents are thrilled that their kids are learning skills and fundamental processes they use every day in their own places of work, like Capital One and the Federal Reserve Bank.

Romeo-Green's program will offer high school students the opportunity to test for CAPM-R (Certified Associate in Project Management) accreditation after graduation. CAPM credentials are often used as a stepping stone to the PMP (Project Management Professional Certification). CAMP and PMP are the most highly recruited and highly compensated in the technology industry. Just think about how this will look on a résumé. Susan adds, "In addition to the above, . . . when individuals in a community receive resources and opportunities like this program provides, your talent pool becomes much stronger, corporations become drawn to the community, and service jobs follow. It's a win, win for everyone". *Flipm* is also assisting high school students with tuition for colleges and universities, providing full four year scholarships.

Thank you, Susan, for permitting me to introduce this awesome program to the nation. Virginia is the first to participate. We will all appreciate, specifically designed to accompany this book, the board game by (TR) Winning the Training Game LLC., Susan Burton. The game is scheduled for release in 2014/2015 for use in churches, schools, and homes around the globe. Look for the interactive training board game, "Let's Make Peace@ Home."

Yet another encounter occurred while searching for a specific color of shoes at Old Navy in Richmond. For some time, I had wanted to connect with Charmaine, one of my wonderful former students. I had seen her mother, Cheryl, many months ago and had gotten a telephone number. I knew I should not have put the number on a piece of paper. I did and I lost it.

On this day, I ran into Cheryl, asked for the number and put it in my address book. I also got Cheryl's number. After our reintroductions she shared her joyous news about her upcoming wedding. As we continued to talk she began to talk about her son, Nigel, who had gone astray, and who now had gotten himself together and had been in recovery for a few months.

I met Nigel, a former student and graduate from the Commonwealth Challenge Academy. Cheryl was overjoyed that Nigel had come through Commonwealth's rigid boot camp and was on his way back into society better than he was before he entered the program.

She introduced him to me and I was surprised at his openness and upbeat personality. He discussed the reason for his new beginning—Commonwealth Challenge Academy. It was started in 1994 at Camp Pendleton, Virginia. There have been 3,000 graduates who are living successful lives. It is located one mile from the beach.

As I listened, I said a quiet prayer that he would always remember where he was and who brought him through. He knew it was God. I see God's hand as He wants mothers, fathers and others to be able to utilize this resource, one that will enable other young boys who have lost their way, to attend Commonwealth Challenge Academy in order that they might reclaim a better future/reach their potential and also help other peers to succeed.

Cheryl, his mother, was teary-eyed as she was remembering where he was when he entered the program and how far he had come. There was hope, believing that Nigel would indeed have a successful future helping others like himself. Cheryl credits Commonwealth Challenge Academy—which states—"A second chance awaits you." It's a 22 week residential program that is structured in a military style environment to promote academics, attendance to detail, time management, and leadership while promoting self-esteem, confidence and pride. It is founded under the Department of Defense. There is no charge to the family for tuition, room, board or books.

Donna O and Y C Chen are two of the persons I encountered. My daughter and I met them as they presented their program, **Guaranteed 4.0 Learning Program System** to a group of parents and grandparents at the home of one of her friends.

We were interested in using the program to enhance our children's and grandchildren's knowledge base. To our surprise the program was easy to follow, and if followed properly, children earn 4.0 grade point averages. These are practical ways to become more organized at home and in college. Check out this masterpiece. www.guaranteed4.0.com

Chenie M. Jordan, M.Ed., of Jordan's Quest, Inc., is a consultant who coaches happy parents by making them aware of the possibilities. Chenie, a parent education consultant, provides parenting classes with resource information and literacy programs. If you live in the Richmond, Virginia area, she will come directly to you. For other areas, contact her at www.jordansquest.com, and at www.cjordanejordansquest.com.

Miriam Owens wrote *Help, Hints, Hope for the Homework Weary.* This book is for all parents who have children that struggle with behaviors at home and school following expected rules. Miriam's book gives strategies, hints, help and hope for homework weary parent that they can follow. Her book is one that supports parents with children with autism. (www.miriamowenz@aol.com/RhemaDesigns.)

Dr. Sheary Johnson founded **The Ministry Connection**, an online, web based data base for your Christian ministry. It was formed after servicing local ministries with their programs' internet service and its needs. It is now a national ministry. (**The Ministry Connection:** Founder Dr. Sheary Johnson: Networking, Training, Mentorship, and resources to Grow and Cultivate your ministry or organization, www.myministryconnection.com. and www.miriamOwenz@aol.com/RhemaDesigns)

References

Bevere, Lisa. *The True Measure of a Woman*. Lake Mary: Charisma House, 1997.

Carson, Ben & Murphy, Cecil. *Think Big Unleashing Your Potential for Excellence*. Grand Rapids: Zondervan, 1997

Canfield, Jack, Hansen, Mark Victor. *Chicken Soup for the Pre-teen's Talk*. Cos Cob: CSS Chicken Soup for the Soul Publishing LLC, 2008.

Canfield, Jack, Hansen, Mark Victor, Newmark, Amy. *Chicken Soup for the Teen's Soul*. Cos Cob: CSS Chicken Soup for the Soul Publishing LLC, 2011.

Canfield, J., Hansen, M. V., McKowen, D., Gardner, J., Gardner, E., Hill, T., & Wilson, Kyle. *Chicken Soup for the Entrepreneur's Soul*. Deer Beach: Health Communications INC, 2006.

Copeland, Germaine. *Prayers that Avail Much for Children*. Tulsa: Harrison House, 1996.

Dobson, James, C. PhD. *Parenting Isn't for Cowards*. Dallas: Word Publishing, 2000.

Dobson, James, C., PhD. *The Strong-Willed Child*. Wheaten: Tyndale House, 1992.

Dollar, Creflo. *8 Steps to Create The Life You Want*. New York, Boston, Nashville: Faith Words, 2002.

Green, Conrad E. *Needed But Not Wanted: Chronological Study of African Americans in America, Part I.* USA: NorthLight Publishing, 2009.

Hicky, Marilyn. *Building Blocks for Better Families.* Denver: Marilyn Hickey Ministries, 1998.

Jakes. T. D. *Mama Made the Difference. Life Lessons My Mother Taught Me.* New York: The Penguin Group, 2006.

Johnson, Sheary D., Ed. D. *Why I Didn't Say Yes: Understanding the Dynamics of the Body, Soul and Spirit.* Columbus: Brentwood Press, 2006.

Kunjusu, Dr. Jawanza, *Raising Black Boys.* Chicago: African American Images, 2007.

Leman, Kevin, Dr. *Have a New Child by Friday: How to Change Your Child's Attitude, Behavior and Character in 5 Days.* Grand Rapids: Revell, 2012.

Leman, Kevin, Dr. *Have a New Teenager by Friday: From Mouthy and Moody to Respect and Responsibility in 5 days.* Grand Rapids: Revell, 2011.

Meyer, Joyce. *Starting Your Day Right: Devotions for Each Morning of the Year.* New York: Zondervan, 1982.

Meyer, Joyce. *The Battlefield of the Mind.* New York Boston Nashville: Faith Words, 2002.

Munroe, Myles. *Potential a daily devotional for Every Day.* Shippensburg: Destiny Image Publishers, INC. 2008.

Omartian, Stormie. *The Power of a Praying Parent.* Eugene: Harvest House, 1995.

Osteen, Joel. *It's Your Time.* New York London Toronto Sydney: Free Press, 2004.

RHT. *It Works. If You Know What You Want You Can Have It.* Camarillo: DeVorss Publishing Company, 2008.

Wilkes, Irene. *Elvie Saves Christmas.* Printed in the U.S.A.: Inkwater Press, 2011.

Winston, Bill. *The Power of the Tongue.* Oak Park: Time Publishing and Media Group, 2002.

About the Author

Patricia Braxton earned a BS in elementary education from Southern Illinois University and earned credits toward a master's degree. Now retired and living in Virginia, she taught elementary school for more than forty years and continues to substitute teach in the Richmond (Virginia) City Public schools. She has also been a teacher trainer around the country.

Cover Copy

Parents serve as their children's first teachers. What they learn at home helps them build on their learning and education at school. In *A Parent's Guide to a Peaceful Home*, Patricia Braxton provides a guide for helping parents manage their homes in peaceful, loving ways in order to ensure success for their children at home and at school.

This handbook presents Braxton's TAD (Towards Affective Development) model, which gives practical advice to help parents teach their children responsibility, respect, discipline, and other positive character traits. It also teaches parents how to relate to each other properly and how to effect change from within.

Through TAD, Braxton works to change the face of families in a positive way. The steps detailed in *A Parent's Guide to a Peaceful Home* can facilitate an atmosphere where love, compassion, respect, and other virtues are taught by example and reinforced to produce a lasting, peaceful home.